LAMBORGHINI

First published in 2004 by Motorbooks International, an imprint of
MBI Publishing Company, Galtier Plaza, Suite 200, 380 Jackson Street,
St. Paul, MN 55101-3885 USA

© David Jolliffe, 2004

All rights reserved. With the exception of quoting brief passages for the purposes of review, no part of this publication may be reproduced without prior written permission from the Publisher.

The information in this book is true and complete to the best of our knowledge. All recommendations are made without any guarantee on the part of the author or Publisher, who also disclaim any liability incurred in connection with the use of this data or specific details.

This publication has been prepared solely by MBI Publishing Company and is not approved or licensed by any other entity. We recognize that some words, model names and designations mentioned herein are the property of the trademark holder. We use them for identification purposes only. This is not an official publication.

Motorbooks International titles are also available at discounts in bulk quantity for industrial or sales-promotional use. For details write to Special Sales Manager at Motorbooks International Wholesalers & Distributors, Galtier Plaza, Suite 200, 380 Jackson Street, St. Paul, MN 55101-3885 USA.

Back cover (left to right): Countach LP 500 S and 350 GTV

LAMBORGHINI
Forty Years

DAVID JOLLIFFE WITH TONY WILLARD

MOTORBOOKS
INTERNATIONAL

Contents

Introduction_Life before Lamborghini — 07

01_One in the eye for the Prancing Horse — 15

02_Torrid times for the Fighting Bull — 35

03_The challenger on its knees — 51

04_Frenchmen mount a rescue — 67

05_Dollars do the talking — 85

06_Coup de grace for Bravo; farewell Chrysler	103
07_ The Brits and Megatech: imperfect harmony	115
08_Audi partner! Four new rings for the fighting bull	133
09_Bullish on the future; back to fighting form	155
Appendix_Technical Specifications	169
Index	188
Acknowledgements	191

"The thrill of the high-speed drive through Europe that followed made me determined to create a career around the finest and fastest cars. For two years, I was to go to Italy to collect cars from Ferrari"

David Jolliffe

Introduction_Life before Lamborghini

My flirtation with Ferrari as a young man later developed into a long and continuing love affair with Lamborghini. What an irony, for it was a dispute with founder Enzo Ferrari that made Ferruccio Lamborghini start his own company designing and manufacturing exotic Italian sports cars.

In the early 1960s, I was working for Rob Walker, a wealthy man who was the most successful privateer in the history of Formula One (his team won 14 races). Walker had decided to branch into GT (grand turismo or grand touring) racing, and I went to the Ferrari factory at Maranello to collect a 250 GT for Stirling Moss, probably the best British driver never to become world motor racing champion.

The thrill of the high-speed drive through Europe that followed made me determined to create a career around the finest and fastest cars. For two years, I was to go to Italy to collect cars from Ferrari and drive them back to Rob Walker Racing in the UK.

On my first visit to Ferrari, I waited for three days until the car was ready, going daily to

Power player: Ferruccio Lamborghini with an early V12 engine developed for the supercars he built after becoming disenchanted with Ferraris.

INTRODUCTION

the works carrying a suitcase packed with $11,000/£5,500 to pay for it. When I at last drove away from Maranello in northern Italy, only 30 hours were left before the car was due to race at Silverstone and I sped through France in the days before high-speed autoroutes, often touching 150mph. I arrived at the circuit minutes before final qualifying and Stirling leapt behind the wheel. On his second lap, in a car that was new to him, he posted pole position and went on to beat the two Ferrari works cars and the rest of the field.

I had already helped Stirling to win a Formula One race. In 1960, I walked from the pits area of the Monaco Grand Prix circuit to stand at the old Gasworks Hairpin and listen to (not watch) him drive past me during practice. I had to judge whether the engine was geared at its peak as he accelerated out of this difficult corner, and then report back to the rest of the team.

I did this at other circuits and my evaluation of the sound of the engine often meant late-night working to change a ratio to produce more top speed or greater acceleration in the intermediate gears. Like many kids, I had dreamt of being the world's greatest racing driver, and never came near it, but at least I once played a real part in the action.

I travelled the world with Walker's F1 team and developed a lifelong passion for fast cars, including 30 heady years selling and distributing Lamborghinis in Britain. Lambo is the bravest and most thrilling car marque of them all and survived despite a catalogue of near disasters at the hands of a succession of owners. Now, I hope, it will remain in the safe hands of Audi.

Automobili Lamborghini roared into my life in the spring of 1964 when I read in *Motor* magazine about the debut of the 350 GT at the Turin motor show. I was still working for Rob Walker but in a very different role – I was general manager of his garage in a village in the southern English county of Wiltshire, selling cars made by Aston Martin, Jaguar and Alfa Romeo. Lamborghini excited me as a new competitor to England's Aston Martin and it came from an area of Italy that I knew well because of trips to Ferrari and other companies involved with the motor industry.

I was brought up in Surrey, the leafy and affluent county west of London, and educated at Ottershaw. The head at this experimental boarding school in Surrey was Arthur Foot, a brother of Michael Foot (once leader of the UK's Labour Party). When I went for my admission interview, I told him I intended to be a motor racing driver and that I saw myself as a budding champion. That was true, he believed me and I was accepted for Ottershaw.

I left school in 1955 aged 16 because I had no desire to continue studying: I wanted to

get on with pursuing a career in motor sport. I discovered the joy of gearboxes and engines standing alongside my father Stan, who owned a garage that sold new Volvos. He had prepared Rob Walker's Delage which was driven by Tony Rolt, who went on to win the Le Mans 24-Hour race with Jaguar.

A few of the right words in his ear about a son keen on motor racing persuaded Rob Walker to take me on. I started as an apprentice at his Ford showroom in Dorking, Surrey, but with the understanding that I was to be seconded to Walker's racing team in a building a few hundred yards away.

At Rob Walker Racing, I quickly moved from 'oily rag' to work with the men preparing the cars. Grand Prix racing was evolving rapidly, with great factory teams like Ferrari, Mercedes, Vanwall, Maserati, Connaught, Gordini, Lotus and Cooper starting to appear on the starting grids. Sponsorship was in its infancy and cars lined up in national colours.

Rob Walker, a great grandson of the Scotch whisky distiller Johnnie Walker, was proud to race his cars in Scotland's midnight blue. In 1957 Walker, together with Cooper Cars, was one of the first to see the potential for placing a Grand Prix car engine at the rear. Walker bought a 1.5-litre Cooper Climax and the engine, positioned at the rear, was increased to 1960cc.

In early 1957, we went to Argentina for the first Grand Prix of the season and as Vanwall had not entered, their driver – Stirling Moss – drove for us. He held off a late

Into production: a promotional shot of the 350 GT *(above)*, the first Lamborghini to meet with Ferruccio's approval and go on sale (120 were built).

Badge of pride: Ferruccio, born under the sign of Taurus, chose the Fighting Bull of Spain *(opposite)* as the symbol for his tractors, and then for high-performance cars.

INTRODUCTION

challenge from the two front-engined Ferraris and, with his tyres down to the canvas, won the race and that marked the beginning of the end for front-engined racing cars. This motor sport revolution was to be adopted by Lamborghini in the mid-1960s, with the rear-engined Miura leading the way.

As a private owner, Rob Walker had to be constantly innovative to remain competitive against cars entered by the manufacturers. I had progressed to being responsible for the gearbox and its ratios, and in those days we used a slide rule to make calculations before fitting the appropriate gear ratios for each circuit from those supplied by Hewland, whose gearboxes were used by Cooper and Lotus. Alf Francis, the chief mechanic, had the inspired thought that the gearbox was the weakest point of our car and carried too much weight. His idea was that the casing should be made in the lightweight alloy Duralumin and that we should cut our own gear ratios to give us a greater choice.

We formed a new company called Colotti Gear Boxes Spa, based in the Modena region of northern Italy (the home of Ferrari and Maserati). Materials were bought in the UK and sent to Modena for machining to Colotti's design. Over the next three years, I was to pay many visits to Modena to work with Colotti on the ratios needed to assemble the gearboxes, and to arrange their transportation back to our base in England. In 1960, when I helped Moss win at Monaco, I was to see the wisdom of Rob Walker's liaison with Colotti.

I had great respect for Colotti and the Modena/Bologna area which was home to legions of stylists and machine shops – it was a Mecca for anyone with a passion for motor sport. At the time though I had no idea that the region was to play such an important role in my future life, as I became close to the senior people at Lamborghini.

I left Rob Walker Racing in 1962 when a series of crashes involving our cars convinced me it was time to change direction. At the Goodwood Easter meeting, Stirling Moss had a major accident and his injuries were so severe they ended his career. This was followed by the deaths in crashes of his replacement drivers – Ricardo Rodriguez, at the Mexican Grand Prix, and then Gary Hocking in South Africa.

Rob Walker was greatly affected by these tragedies and it was only after much consideration that he decided to continue with his Formula One team. His greatest achievement was probably winning the 1966 British Grand Prix at Silverstone with Joe Siffert driving his Lotus 49 in the familiar midnight blue livery.

In 1964 I was to achieve my childhood dream and drove a racing car competitively. Walker also owned a Ford dealership and as the Lotus Cortina was Ford powered the

"I had no idea that the region was to play such an important role in my future life, as I became close to the senior people at Lamborghini"

manufacturer persuaded him to take a racing Lotus Cortina and enter it for a season of British saloon car racing. There was no room for it at Rob's racing base and I needed little persuasion to have the car based at my garage, with instructions to keep a watching brief over the project.

The Cortina's first race was in spring 1964 and John Fenning, a Lotus works Formula Junior driver, was contracted to drive it. I was already at Goodwood when I received a message from the organisers that Fenning had been injured in an accident on the way to the circuit and was in hospital. On phoning Rob Walker, who had stayed at home, it was decided that as I had tested the car and held a provisional race licence that I should take the wheel in the race. I did reasonably well and with John out for some months it was agreed that I should drive the car for the rest of the season.

I won some club races but was soon to learn that beating Jim Clark and Graham Hill in works-prepared Lotus Cortinas at international events was beyond my abilities. Clark gave great support in practice but once the race was underway he disappeared into the distance, hotly pursued by Graham Hill. After one year the commitment to the Lotus

Hands on: working at Rob Walker Racing brought respect later for Ferruccio (left), who kept a close watch on what was happening in his production area.

INTRODUCTION

Cortina ended and my involvement in racing car preparation was over. I did though drive a Mini Cooper S for Janspeed Engineering.

I came to accept that business life must come first, and in 1966 leased a small garage with an Alfa Romeo franchise in west London. I was elected to the dealer council, which looked after the interests of people selling new Alfa Romeos, and became friends with Mario Condivi, who had a contract to distribute Alfas in Britain.

The Italian held the lease on the building but wanted to move to larger premises. This was a great opportunity for me and, with some financial help from my father, I left Rob Walker after 11 years to start my own company, trading from Condivi's original dealership as Portman Garages, selling Alfas, and later Lancias. At the time, Lancia was independent from Fiat, the biggest Italian car manufacturer, and had a gem of a model called the Fulvia.

I now had connections with two Italian car makers, but the ambition to sell supercars was getting stronger. It was not long before I met Roger Philips, managing director of the Lamborghini importer in Britain. I told him I wanted to be Lamborghini's London dealer.

In the summer of 1972, I was with a group of UK Alfa Romeo dealers checking-in for a flight back to London after a factory visit. Roger Philips, who was with Walter Woolf, a wealthy businessman and Lamborghini enthusiast, spotted me by chance. Woolf had his executive jet at the airport and I was invited to join them on a flight to Lamborghini's plant, where Woolf was to finalise the specification of his Miura.

This was my first of more than 100 visits in the coming years to the factory at Sant'Agata Bolognese, a small town about 15 miles north of Bologna in northern Italy.

On that first visit, three people made a huge impression on me, especially Ferruccio Lamborghini, the founder of the company, because I quickly realised the importance of his personal involvement in the development of the cars.

During a guided tour of the plant, Roger and I went to a toilet in the engineering area (literally, a hole in the ground that we stood around). We were one each side of a man who I assumed was just one of the team. Then Roger was speaking: 'Ferruccio, I would like you to meet David Jolliffe who wants to sell Lamborghinis in Britain.'

Ferruccio turned towards me and offered his spare hand to shake, which I did. I then looked down and realised my shoes were wet; it was an odd but unforgettable baptism from a man whose vision and determination were to become such an important part in my life.

The second man to earn my immediate respect was Ubaldo Sgarzi, responsible for sales and with an enthusiasm for all things Lamborghini that knew no bounds. The third

was Paolo Stanzani who could not stop talking of Lamborghini's engineering ambitions. I have kept in touch with Sgarzi and we remain good friends.

As my Lamborghini business grew, and I later became UK distributor, I watched the manufacturer endure trauma after trauma at the hands of a string of owners.

Ferruccio Lamborghini's early vision produced a car marque of undeniable spirit. He died in 1993, shortly before his 76th birthday, at a time Lamborghini's future was yet again in doubt.

A little over a decade after his passing, it is time to tell the real story of both Lamborghinis - the man and his company - and this book was written in partnership with Tony Willard, an automotive journalist and writer. The story is about the vision, passion and dedication of Ferruccio and the small band of people persuaded to join him on a great adventure.

Ferruccio was born under the star sign of Taurus the bull, and chose the bravest breed of bull as a badge of pride for his cars because he wanted Lamborghini to trample on the prancing horse, the symbol of Ferrari.

The fortunes of Lamborghini have fluctuated during its first 40 years but now, with Audi and the Volkswagen group in charge, the Fighting Bull may yet fulfil Ferruccio's dream by becoming more successful than Ferrari.

David Jolliffe *May 2004.*

Fighting Bull: an early photograph of Ferruccio at his desk *(above)* - **his hunched shoulders and steady gaze indicated a man ready for the struggles ahead.**

Applying the shine: after all the hard work during development, the 350 GT *(left)* **was put into a glamorous setting for marketing photographs to appeal to customers.**

"He was a natural engineer, and saw the chance to convert army trucks into agricultural equipment. That business – and another making air conditioning units – created the wealth that enabled Ferruccio to make sports cars that would challenge Enzo Ferrari's."

01_One in the eye for the Prancing Horse

F erruccio Lamborghini had a strong handshake, powerful build, broad shoulders and the perfect human form of the fighting bull used in his company logo. If ever a man looked as though he was born under the sign of Taurus, it was this one. He was a man of the soil from a family that had been farmers for many generations.

Bright and clever, he saw a great business opportunity at the end of World War II. Italy was left with a huge number of trucks and other military equipment, most of it destined for the scrap heap. He was a natural engineer, and saw the chance to convert army trucks into agricultural equipment. That business – and another making air conditioning units – created the wealth that enabled Ferruccio to make sports cars that would challenge Enzo Ferrari's.

Lamborghini the man was born on April 28, 1916, in the small agricultural town of Renazza di Cento in the northern Italian province of Emilia. The flat and fertile land of the area is farming country, extending from the great River Po south to the Adriatic (an area popularly referred to as the Po Valley). This was a major gateway for the industrialised cities of Turin and Milan.

Crowd pleaser: after making an impression among motor show visitors, the 350 GT soon became the centre of attention wherever it was seen in northern Italy.

CHAPTER 01

As a teenager, Ferruccio became interested in the equipment used in the local farming community, and persuaded his parents to allow him to enrol in a technical college to study engineering. World War II was to curtail his studies and he joined the Italian Air Force, working in the logistics department that supplied parts to maintain aircraft and support vehicles.

Ferruccio was stationed with the ground crew on the Greek island of Rhodes and had a chance to hone his skills in mechanical improvisation. After the fall of the island at the end of the war in 1945, Ferruccio was held as a prisoner of the British until he was allowed to return home the following year.

Down to business: Ferruccio was at his happiest discussing technical points on the shop floor of his factory *(above)*.

Field of vision: Ferruccio sits on the bonnet of a Jarama 400 GT *(left)* – one of the supercars financed by the success of his tractor business.

Italy, in common with the rest of Europe, had a desperate shortage of civilian machinery. The country had made the war effort the priority for its industrial and agricultural output and car plants had been neglected, or in some cases literally blitzed.

Ferruccio looked at the various business opportunities and in 1947 decided he could source materials to allow him to improvise machinery for the farming community.

In the same year, he modified an old Fiat Topolino, increasing the engine size to 750cc to improve its performance, to compete in Italy's Mille Miglia road race in 1948. With 700 miles of the race behind them, Ferruccio and his co-driver careered off the road. The two men escaped unscathed but Ferruccio lost his enthusiasm for motor racing – a change of heart that was to influence crucial decisions at his car plant in the future.

By 1949 war surplus materials were proving more difficult to find, but Ferruccio was bouyed by his success with the equipment he had already supplied. His knowledge of the agricultural marketplace persuaded him to establish a tractor manufacturing company

CHAPTER 01

(Lamborghini Tractori Spa) at Cento in his heartland. The venture was to prove a great success, with both production and profitability growing over the next 20 years. His tractors, painted black and white, became a familiar sight and bore what was to be his famous logo, the Fighting Bull.

Ferruccio's competitive edge, and instinctive ability to command attention, gave him the idea of staging tugs-of-war between his tractors and others in the surrounding market towns. In this way, he demonstrated the superiority of his products.

Over the course of the next decade, Ferruccio concentrated on developing his business making and selling tractors. Then, in 1960, he seized on another business opportunity - the growing demand for heating and air conditioning systems from an Italian industry in renaissance - and established Lamborghini Bruciatori.

With his two factories, he enjoyed both fame and wealth and took full advantage of the tax breaks given to start-up industries in post-war Italy. As a relatively young man (his 30th birthday was in 1946), Ferruccio was established and successful in the region's business and social life but he was not yet fully satisfied, and explored many other projects over the next decade.

By then, he was also able to ignite his love of cars and bought (among others) a Ferrari, a Jaguar and a Mercedes. Legend has it that, as a local industrialist, he was dissatisfied with the Ferraris he purchased because he felt the aftersales service was not up to standard. Ferruccio also criticised Ferrari's product range as essentially track cars that were, as road cars, too noisy and intractable. He believed the cabins lacked the build quality that a customer had the right to expect.

Legend, never denied by Ferruccio, has it that he sought a meeting with Enzo Ferrari to discuss his dissatisfaction - businessman to businessman, with a shared interest in the region's commercial development. Ferruccio had no direct response and a phone call from someone in Enzo's office was interpreted as a snub by Ferruccio who then convinced himself there was a market for a sports car that would appeal to people like himself - wealthy and demanding the best.

The Ferruccio vision was of a grand turismo with a powerful and tractable power unit, driver and passenger comfort, beautifully appointed interiors, a quiet and good-quality ride and an effective braking system. If Enzo Ferrari was not prepared to listen to this, reasoned Ferruccio, he might build such a car himself.

He began to explore the possibilities of starting his third company to manufacture luxury

First born: the Lamborghini 350 GTV during prototype testing - Ferruccio decided it was not good enough to carry the badge of the Fighting Bull.

On the street: the 350 GT was a familiar sight on the streets of Sant'Agata *(above)*, where magazine photographers found perfect backdrops for the car.

Special order: a Miura V12 *(right)*, tuned by Lamborghini's Bob Wallace, was used in this racing car, built in Bologna for an enthusiast in Salt Lake City, Utah.

GT cars carrying his name. In 1962, using experience acquired through setting up Lamborghini Tractori and Lamborghini Bruciatori, he found land at Sant'Agata Bolognese, about 15 miles north of Bologna. The political climate of the day in the area favoured his plans.

The city's Communist party leadership wanted to encourage manufacturers to establish new plants and so create jobs, and the Modena/Bologna area already had industrial strength through specialist car makers like Ferrari, Maserati and Stangallini, plus the supporting infrastructure of machine shops, styling houses, chassis builders and race car manufacturers.

Awaiting a call from the ambitious Ferruccio was a nucleus of trained engineers, and he was later able to exploit this to the full. He negotiated attractive financial terms to build the job-creating factory at Sant'Agata and they included an agreement to pay no tax on the plant's profits during its first 10 years of trading.

Displaying his flair for good business, Ferruccio won a dream of a deal with the authorities. He was given an interest-free loan and would be able to deposit any cash generated by his start-up car manufacturing company in an account that would pay an interest rate of 19 per cent. As part of the arrangement, he had to make payroll employees members of Italy's powerful sheetmetal workers' union. This would make it extremely difficult for Ferruccio to shed staff without closing down the business.

By the end of 1962, Ferruccio had started work on the first stage of the factory, laying down a production line and a machine shop facility capable of building engines together with test equipment. With an initial investment of $350,000/£175,000, in part his own money but part also cash taken from his existing businesses, he was able to start production in 1963.

To fulfil his dream, Ferruccio knew he had to recruit with great care and his top priority was to build a strong engineering team - men who were already considered distinguished or at least displayed special talents. It was typical of the man that he never hesitated to go head-hunting for the people he identified as essential to his requirements. At that time, it was normal for specialist car manufacturers to source bodyshells from specialist builders, but to design and manufacture all the moving parts, including the engine and transmission. Then the car manufacturer completed the final assembly, and was responsible for overall quality.

CHAPTER 01

From the moment he decided to build exotic sports cars, Ferruccio knew he wanted to employ the visionary engineer Giotto Bizzarrini who, as a young man, had already worked with Alfa Romeo on its V12 engine. Bizzarrini was an integral part of Ferrari where he worked on the legendary 250 GTO.

After enjoying a couple of excellent dinners with Ferruccio, Bizzarrini found the prospect of joining Automobili Ferruccio Lamborghini with a clean sheet of paper – and a brief to design a 3.5-litre V12 engine at a new facility – utterly irresistible. Ferruccio would not have been human if he had not experienced a sense of extra satisfaction knowing he had robbed Enzo Ferrari (the man he felt had snubbed him) of such a vital engineer.

Bizzarrini and Ferruccio set about welding together the most talented team of engineers possible, and two of them (again young, but already enjoying incredible reputations) were head-hunted, again from Ferrari. Giampaolo Dallara and Paolo Stanzani joined a group of people who were destined to excite the world with their cars.

Basing himself at the tractor plant at Cento, Bizzarrini set to work to design a 3.5-litre, 60-degree V12 engine with four overhead camshafts, aluminium block and steel liners. The 60-degree angle was seen as the best to provide perfect balance and reduce vibration to a minimum.

A British motoring writer of some standing has always maintained that the engine was not all Bizzarrini's own work. LJK Setright, a devoted believer in the engineering prowess of Honda, believes he based the design on one of the Japanese company's Formula One engines.

In his book *Legendary Car Engines* (also published by Motorbooks International), John Simister records the Setright theory, and confirms similarities between the two engines, but is inclined to side with the official version.

> Simister, referring to the similarities, writes: "The script says that Giotto Bizzarrini originally created a very similar design, but with a capacity of just 1.5 litres, as a design study for a Formula One engine. Tractor maker Ferruccio Lamborghini, casting around for a power unit able to match, or preferably exceed, anything which Ferrari was offering in a road car, then commissioned Bizzarrini to enlarge his neat V12 for Lamborghini's proposed GT. Job done.
>
> But there's a shadowy subtext to this, denied by those who have to stay on-message but intriguing enough to be exhumed here. The weight of opinion is firmly against any notion that Lamborghini's V12 was

> "So Lamborghini decided he would trump Ferrari's 1950s-designed efforts with an engine more powerful and more sophisticated than anything yet seen in a roadgoing supercar" - **author John Simister**

Engineering success: Ferruccio *(left)* knew from the start that he wanted to employ Ferrari's Giotto Bizzarrini, who was to design the legendary Lamborghini V12.

created by Honda, but maverick British motoring journalist (and total Honda fan) LJK Setright was adamant, in a story for *Supercar Classics* magazine in 1986, that this was the case. His argument was compelling, and took advantage of the natural modesty and business ethics of the Japanese who would never admit to their involvement if they had been asked not to.

Look at Honda's exquisite 1.5-litre V12 Formula One engine of 1965, and you can see the similarities. One of the more unusual features of Lamborghini's V12, albeit not unique because a similar idea was used by BMW in the pre-war 328 and various race-engine designers since, is that the inlet ports are between the overhead camshafts that top each bank of six cylinders. Normally a vee-engine feeds its cylinders from between the arms of the vee or, less commonly, from the outer sides with the exhausts emerging within the vee. But not here.

Why? If you use vertical carburettors, as did the Miura, then it's a fairly straight inlet tract: just a 30-degree bend given the vee-angle of 60 degrees. It also made it possible to use regular sidedraught Weber DCOEs, not normally found on a vee-engine, albeit with a bit of a dog-leg in the pipework. The Espada engine is thus equipped. So, if we ask why, the reply could just as easily be: why not?

Here, though, we'll stick with the authorised version. Ferruccio Lamborghini, having owned several Ferraris, reckoned that the machines from Maranello could easily be improved upon. And having suffered problems with both his Ferraris and the aftersales back-up, he vowed to beat Maranello at its own game.

In particular, he thought, Ferrari's road engines were a little old-fashioned with their single-cam heads. So Lamborghini decided he would trump Ferrari's 1950s-designed efforts with an engine more powerful and more sophisticated than anything yet seen in a roadgoing supercar: a four-cam V12 with a short stroke and a big racing pedigree in its conception.

Bizzarrini, in a past life the project leader for Ferrari's exquisite 250 GTO, came up with a proposal which appealed very strongly to the entrepreneurial Ferruccio. He would accept no payment for the engine

CHAPTER 01

design alone; rather he would be paid by the brake horsepower achieved above that of Ferrari's contemporary 3.0-litre V12. Inevitably this could lead to a race-specification screamer rather than the well-mannered GT motor that Lamborghini wanted, but it would undeniably show the potential locked within. The design, now radically enlarged from its on-paper 1.5 litres to a real 3.5, was finished off and refined for the road. On 15 May 1963, in a corner of the tractor factory because the high-tech, squeaky-clean car plant hadn't been built yet, the V12 burst into life for the first time."

Bizzarrini's 3.5-litre, 60-degree V12 configuration has remained at the heart of top-of-the-range Lamborghinis (today's Murciélago has a 6.2-litre engine, but the basic design is the same). It was not in his brief but Bizzarrini designed the engine in a way that ensured it had a racing potential. Ferruccio was not informed of this aspiration and so was surprised by the power the engine generated on its first test bed running. This was the beginning of what was to become constant conflict between the boss's philosophies for his cars, and those of the engineering teams he created.

The final configuration was 3497cc, with a 9.5 to 1 compression ratio developing an output of 360bhp, making it more powerful than any of Lamborghini's perceived competitors.

From the start, Ferruccio had in mind his first GT and surprisingly decided to commission Franco Scaglione, who ran his own styling studio, to fashion the lines to Lamborghini's instructions. Scaglione was not well known and he seemed a surprising choice. He was though respected by European car makers for his work and once the styling was agreed, the race was on to get the body built in a few months.

The car, designated 350 GTV, had to be ready for the 1963 Turin motor show, which gave the team four months to complete it. The urgency of the project had presumably excluded Vignale, Ghia, Bertone and other internationally-respected stylists. Pininfarina, which had a close association with Ferrari and Fiat, was always rejected by Ferruccio as a stylist. Once he had approved the styling, Scaglione worked in close collaboration with Sargiotto Bodyworks of Turin. The car was completed by Lamborghini and Sargiotto just in time for the show and the 350 GTV – the first Lamborghini – was announced to the world.

Ferruccio, heartened by the warm reception from journalists and other Turin show visitors, reviewed the work carried out by Scaglione and Sargiotto. He liked the styling,

Heading for the heights: praise for the 350 GT encouraged Ferruccio to press on and build cars including the Miura, seen here during testing on mountain roads.

CHAPTER 01

which had largely followed his brief, but said the build quality was unacceptable. He was careful to make clear that he was pleased with his own team's efforts on the engine and transmission, as the car was both powerful and quiet.

Ferruccio reluctantly decided the show car was no more than a one-off concept, and could not go into production carrying his name and logo.

This was not the start he had hoped for, and the prototype was put into storage where it remained for 20 years. It was then fully and faithfully restored by Emilianauto of Bologna, a Lamborghini dealership, for a local collector, Romano Bernardoni.

In 1963, Ferruccio decided to make a fresh start on the quest for a body that he felt did justice to the excellence of the mechanical components, and Touring Bodyworks of Milan was commissioned to restyle Scaglione's 350 GTV. Later, he was to work with Bertone.

At the time, Touring was a household name and its clients included Alfa Romeo, Aston Martin, Ferrari, Maserati and Lancia. Ferruccio became optimistic again, saying he wanted the new model to debut at the 1964 Geneva motor show.

Construction of the chassis was taken in-house by Lamborghini and reworked largely on the lines of the 350 GTV's original. Following road tests, minor changes were made to the engine, which had slightly reduced brake horsepower to give sweeter driving characteristics.

The dry sump engine (largely a racing practice) was dropped in favour of a wet sump and other mechanical features that would reduce production costs were introduced despite Bizzarrini's disapproval. Touring's revamp was most noticeable at the front of the car, and Ferruccio approved the overall effect of the exercise. He was much happier with the build quality this time, and the car - badged 350 GT - made its appearance on time in the spring of 1964 at the Geneva show. The changes to the original styling were minor but made an impact on the motoring press and potential customers. Lamborghini was starting to earn respect.

Ferruccio had sensed that his car project would be a success the second time around and, in time for Geneva, had recruited Ubaldo Sgarzi to head the sales department. Sgarzi had worked in a similar position with Italian manufacturer Tecno Spa and seen its effective bankruptcy caused by the pressure on its finances from competing in Formula One racing.

Sgarzi's opposition to involvement in Formula One was in tune with Ferruccio's reluctance to consider motor racing or evolve road cars that were close to circuit sports cars. The two men remained united on this aspect of the business, though Ferruccio's

Close-up: the engine compartment of the 400 GT (right), and a glimpse inside the cabin of the Miura.

stance was to continually bring him into conflict with many of the brilliant engineers who were to work at Lamborghini through Sgarzi's 30 years with the company.

Interest generated at the Geneva show convinced Ferruccio that he could finally commence production and cars were built for 13 customers by the end of 1964. In the remarkably short time of two years, he had conceived and built a factory that was building and selling desirable sports cars.

The launch price of the 350 GT was not a true reflection of build costs but Ferruccio pressed on. He was mindful of the Ferrari 275, which was more powerful than the Lamborghini, and encouraged Giampaolo Dallara to develop a bigger and more powerful version of Bizzarrini's 3.5-litre engine. With its size increased to 3929cc, the engine gave 320bhp at 6,500rpm and was the power source for the next Lamborghini, the 400 GT. This car was designed to be sold alongside the 350 GT, which was to continue in production for a further two years (120 were built).

The 400 GT, also built by Touring, had a longer chassis than the first car and there was more room in the cockpit. First orders were taken in 1965, with deliveries starting the following year. This was a popular car that was totally faithful to Ferruccio's philosophy. Lamborghini built a total of 250 400 GTs and by 1966 the labour force at the factory had risen to 170, with 40 of them working in research and development.

CHAPTER 01

Then Ferruccio began to cast his net more widely to find the senior people he wanted. His head-hunters approached an engineer working for Maserati, a popular New Zealander called Bob Wallace, who became the first non-Italian to enter the inner circle at Lamborghini. His special skill was an ability to road test a car, and then feed back to engineers like Dallara and Stanzani all they needed to know before addressing handling, braking or other problems.

By January, 1965, the top team at Lamborghini was in confident mood. Ferruccio was eager to maintain the pace of progress, and the year was to see collaboration for the first time with Zagato. The chassis and moving parts of the 400 GT were sent to Zagato's coachworks in Turin where a team completed the engineering and construction programme. In the autumn, Zagato's interpretation of the 400 GT made an appearance at the Paris motor show to test public reaction. Zagato had established a reputation for very distinctive styling while working for Alfa Romeo and, in particular, Aston Martin.

Ferruccio was now facing an important decision. There were obvious advantages in paying a specialist coachbuilder to complete cars but he wanted to make the most of his own factory and employees. Ferruccio was proud of what Lamborghini had achieved, and became convinced that the 400 GT should be its core model. He was full of admiration for the Zagato styling but the model was dropped.

Two Zagato prototypes were sold and are now among the rarest and most prized car collectors' pieces. Lamborghini maintained an interest in keeping a link with outside coachbuilders and Touring produced a convertible version of the 350 GTS.

During 1965, Sant'Agata was driven mainly by the genius of Giampaolo Dallara and Lamborghini invested in equipment to increase the production of engines, transmissions and other components. The other strand of Ferruccio's strategy was the construction of an aftersales facility to give owners complete back-up, and somewhere they could take cars for anything from a major rebuild to a minor service. As a man who loved high-quality cars, Ferruccio was aware of the importance of providing continuing service to owners.

In fact, 1965 changed Lamborghini's position in the supercar league: it was the year Dallara drew the sensational Miura, though the car was to begin life as P400, a motor show concept model. Dallara, Stanzani and Wallace – working largely in their own time – had a revolutionary concept for a road-going sports car born out of their deep passion for motor racing. They wanted to transfer technology developed to win on the track to sports cars enthusiasts could drive on public roads.

> "Working late into the night, the three men evolved a design for an endurance event sports car, believing they could convince Ferruccio it would have the potential to be a winner"

And there was a hidden agenda. Working late into the night, the three men evolved a design for an endurance event sports car, believing they could convince Ferruccio it would have the potential to be a winner.

Ferruccio, of course, had already made it clear that such a project was both too costly and would be a distraction: it was not something Lamborghini would do. Dallara, enthused by his radical new design, went to Ferruccio and argued his case for the Miura to be given a budget to prepare a prototype. It was to have a Lamborghini chassis and major mechanical components, and Bertone would be responsible for styling.

To his amazement, Ferruccio gave the project a tentative go-ahead, but he was viewing the car in an entirely different way. He imagined it as a potent marketing device to attract publicity for Lamborghini at international motor shows and other events. Ferruccio believed this would enhance the marque's reputation for innovative engineering and the most unusual technical aspect of the P400/Miura was its rear-mounted engine, a first for Lamborghini. Almost all the knowledge relating to rear engines lay with companies participating in Grand Prix racing and Dallara set to work with a clean piece of paper to design a new chassis.

Dallara did not have the luxury of a free hand and Ferruccio insisted that he used the Bizzarrini 4-litre engine. The designer wanted the model to be small and light and was convinced the only way to retain chassis rigidity was to stiffen the whole car. To accomplish this, he created a structure based on a wide central tunnel with two side lateral elements joined by the floor plate and upper reinforcing structures. The central box section was then extended forward and rearward by boxed trapezoid arms lengthened to the suspension points. These components were lightened by holes where possible and Dallara accommodated the power unit by turning the engine transversely and placing it behind the driver.

Dallara had to find places for the transmission and differential despite the lack of space. He and Stanzani decided that changes were essential and their solution was the most difficult – a single one-off casting bolted directly to the engine, effectively making all three components one unit.

This work was undertaken at Sant'Agata which had the expertise to produce these intricate castings. Such was the enthusiasm within the factory that the chassis and engine were exhibited at the 1965 Turin motor show to show off Lamborghini's engineering prowess to rivals, owners and potential customers. The Miura was to debut in 1966.

CHAPTER 01

Ferruccio was determined not to repeat the mistake of the 350 GTV styling although he was won over by his team's engineering skills. Bertone of Turin was instructed to undertake the styling of the P400 and the timing was most fortuitous. Dallara and Stanzani were both under 30 and Bertone had just employed a young styling genius, Marcello Gandini. Under the watchful eye of the two patrons, Dallara and Gandini were instructed to collaborate and the whole project was to be moved rapidly so that P400 could be on the stand at the 1966 Geneva motor show.

The Miura was completed with days to spare and painted a vibrant orange but the tight schedule created a major problem. No one had found time to compare the size of the engine with the compartment into which it was supposed to fit. The engine was too big and by then all were committed to showing the car.

With an empty engine compartment, the car would not sit at the right height on the stand and the solution was to place ballast in the space. That meant it was essential to keep the P400's engine compartment locked throughout the show, causing sales boss Ubaldo Sgarzi much embarrassment when requested by the world's motoring press to reveal the engine and transmission.

Though lacking an engine, the Miura was visually compelling and many journalists rated it the star of the show. Marcello Gandini, credited with the design and shape, became

Bright prospect: the Miura (the SV version is pictured above and opposite) was painted vibrant orange for its debut at the 1966 Geneva motor show.

a star in his own right. Just before the Geneva show, Bertone, Ferruccio, Dallara and Sgarzi had met to discuss the possible production of the Miura, assuming there was favourable reaction at Geneva. The four men agreed to write on a small piece of paper the number of Miuras that Lamborghini could sell over the next 12 months. Ferruccio (realistic as well as enthusiastic) wrote 20, Sgarzi the salesman 50, designer Dallara 100 and Nuccio Bertone only five. Bertone was to say later that he was not convinced the market place was yet ready for so radical a design.

The name Miura came from one of the most savage breeds of fighting bull, bred by Don Eduardo Miura to fight and almost certainly die in the ring. Miura was the first of a series of Lamborghini names that were to form a link with bulls, breeders or other associations with the art of bull fighting. They were all true to Taurean Ferruccio's fighting bull logo.

The 1966 Geneva motor show was a big success for Lamborghini, because of the accolades showered on Miura and the 400 GT. Ferruccio was content because the 400 GT fulfilled his ambition to build a sophisticated road car, and the Miura suggested his company was innovative and a market leader in the world of supercars.

There were enough orders (secured with deposits) to underwrite the factory's 1967 build and development programme and, with his two other companies also prospering, it was a joyful time for Ferruccio.

He was in harmony with his engineers and other senior colleagues over most aspects of the business, but had to continue to stand his ground over the question of producing a car for racing.

At the end of 1966, he had to tell his team categorically that Lamborghini would not even explore the possibilities of developing Miura for racing. There would come a time when Lamborghini felt it was right to go motor racing, and no one will know whether Ferruccio preserved the company in the 1960s and 1970s or denied it greater fame.

"Lamborghini appeared to be stable and flourishing but had not yet achieved the maturity of Ferrari"

02_Torrid times for the Fighting Bull

Factory expansion at Sant'Agata started in early 1966 and it was completed by the turn of the year when the workforce had increased to nearly 300. Painted and trimmed bodyshells from Touring and Bertone were shipped to the plant for assembly and the number of Miuras to be built was increased to more than 100.

The first four Miuras remained at the factory to be used for development by Bob Wallace who wanted to find ways of improving the model as Lamborghini continued to put the emphasis on quality and refinement. Wallace's changes were built into the cars as they were manufactured and by December of the following year 108 had been delivered to customers. Lamborghini appeared to be stable and flourishing but had not yet achieved the maturity of Ferrari, which built its first road car (the 125 Sport) in 1946, making it 18 years more experienced than Ferruccio's company.

The 400 GT was more fully developed so that production ran smoothly and the factory achieved the planned output of 147 cars, plus three 350 Roadsters. Ferruccio also turned

Battling alone: when business life became tough, Ferruccio (gesturing) found that his son Tonino (with striped tie, to his right) lacked his father's passion for car manufacturing.

CHAPTER 02

his mind to a successor to the 400 GT, and Touring designed a possible replacement on a 400 GT chassis, which they renamed Flying Star. Touring, enduring speculation about its viability, prepared a badly finished vehicle that was rejected by Lamborghini. Another prototype, using an old 350 GT chassis, was built by Neri and Bonacini, a coach-building company in Modena. This well-balanced car was named by the stylist as the Monza 400, but Ferruccio was not convinced the company was large enough to enter into a production commitment. Touring's prototype Flying Star has been bought and sold by collectors and is believed to be privately owned in the UK. The Neri/Bonacini 400 Monza was sold to an enthusiast in the USA.

In 1967, Touring collapsed under mounting financial difficulties and Ferruccio was forced to hand the construction of the Flying Star to a group of former employees headed by Mario Marazzi. Lamborghini model development continued apace that year with Bertone turning its design studio over to a replacement for the 400 GT. The studio was galvanised by the success of Miura and aware of Ferruccio's desire for a high performance four-seat grand tourer.

Working largely alone, but with some support from the engineers at Sant'Agata, Bertone's Marcello Gandini designed a radical new four-seater named the Marzal. The chassis, designed and built at Bertone, was essentially a stretched version of the Miura. Lamborghini's V12 was too big to fit into the bay located at the rear and so one half of the block was used as an inline six-cylinder 2-litre, fitted transversely behind the rear wheels. This way, Gandini was able to accommodate four passengers, with a pair of large gullwing doors allowing access to front and rear seats. Compromises forced on car designers can prove disastrous and once road-testing began, the Marzal was found to have awful road holding.

Gandini incorporated many other innovative design features into the car including the dashboard and the large windows. The car was presented to Ferruccio who was not convinced that the Marzal was a viable replacement for the 400 GT, and it became no more than a motor show exhibit for Lamborghini and Bertone.

The Marzal's greatest claim to fame was an appearance before the start of the 1967 Monaco Grand Prix when it carried Prince Rainier of Monaco and his wife Princess Grace (the former Hollywood actress, Grace Kelly) around the circuit.

Ferruccio pressed on with his collaboration with Mario Marazzi who came up with a design far less radical than the Marzal. This car, destined to go into production in 1968 named Islero, was designed in-house, but in association with Marazzi's coach builders. The

Cool car: the doors of a 400 GT *(above)* are opened before an inspection and test drive on a warm day at the Lamborghini factory.

Lamborghini hospitality: Paolo Stanzani (right) greets a visitor to Sant'Agata while Ferruccio (centre) joins in the joke. *(left)*

hand of Ferrucio remained firmly on styling direction, and the car looked – and indeed was – a direct descendant of the 400 GT.

Bertone then persuaded Ferruccio to allow it to design a new four-seater GT. Following his demand that the GT must use the V12 front engine, a new design came from the pen of Gandini, and an unpainted bodyshell was delivered to Lamborghini, still retaining two very large gullwing doors. Ferruccio insisted that the doors had to be replaced by a conventional pair, and that the car should be equipped with traditional folding front seats.

Bertone produced revised workings and the car was named Espada after matador or toreador, Spain's heroic figure who faces fighting bulls in the ring. The model was to become a significant success for Lamborghini, with total production topping 1,200. Overall, 1966 to 1969 were great years for the factory, and this was the crucial period when Lamborghini established a worldwide reputation. It was selling cars before they were built, and at realistic prices, producing a helpful cash flow through banking customers' deposits.

Most importantly, research and development was proceeding at a frantic pace. In the 1960s, a car's development continued throughout its production life. If body styling, suspension or engine capacity changed, then so did the model prefix.

In 1968, Lamborghini presented the second model that was to cement the global

CHAPTER 02

mystique of the marque. At the Bertone works, following the rejection of the Marzal and the new Espada, work continued using conventional doors and with the two companies collaborating closely.

Lamborghini was able to complete the definitive version in time for its debut at the 1968 Geneva motor show. At the time, the lakeside Swiss city staged Europe's premier motor show, attracting press from around the world, and the Espada 400 GT was widely acclaimed. It was powered by Lamborghini's stock 3929cc, V12, 60-degree twin overhead cam engine, producing 325bhp at 6500 revs.

At this time, the relationship between Ferruccio and Bertone was so cordial that the business relationship between the companies became a little lackadaisical, and the question of ownership of the copyright on the various Lamborghini designs badged by Bertone was never fully established.

This was to cause a major conflict between Bertone and Chrysler, later to become the owner of Lamborghini. The Espada was a success and orders were placed at the Geneva show, encouraging Lamborghini to start production. The Espada, in its three definitive versions, was to stay in production for the next 10 years and 1,217 were built.

Over the years, many journalists have written lyrically about Lamborghinis but few can match these words by Mel Nichols, writing about the Espada in the UK 's *Wheels* magazine in April 1972: 'With the windows lowered, the beat of the four exhausts becomes like a cello backed by an exquisite string orchestra composed by the six combustions occuring on each turn of the crankshaft, the whisper of the chains driving the four crankshafts and the chatter of the 24 valves. This is music, and all of those who love automobiles must sit and listen a few moments before driving off....'.

The Islero, the updated version of the 400 GT designed by Mario Marazzi, was announced in 1968 but destined never to make the same sort of impact in the market as the Espada. Its heritage was clearly evident and the car was welcomed by Lamborghini lovers with much less enthusiasm.

Because of its road characteristics, the Islero enjoyed the support of Ferruccio as it epitomised the type of grand turismo product he enjoyed driving. Its components were thoroughly tested and, with reliability virtually guaranteed, Ferruccio gave the production go-ahead after the Geneva show. Over the next 15 months, 125 Isleros were sold, with the Miura P400 S (usually called the Miura S) arriving in 1968. This version had a stiffer chassis, new Pirelli tyres and power increased to 370bhp (25bhp more than the first Miura) at 7000rpm.

"At this time, the relationship between Ferruccio and Bertone was so cordial that the business relationship between the companies became a little lackadaisical"

On parade: crowds greet the Marzal (top picture) at the 1967 Monaco Grand Prix where it carried Prince Rainier and Princess Grace around the circuit. A 400 GT is seen in close up.

Another significant Miura was to appear at the 1968 Brussels motor show – the Miura P400 Roadster. This was more than an open-top version of a coupe, as Gandini carried out considerable subtle restyling – he was by now effectively head of styling at Bertone. Much effort was directed at the inherent problems of airflow over soft-top cars resulting in buffeting within the cockpit and lack of insulation from road noise.

To combat this, alterations included a restyled rear, new louvres and other detail changes, all made with a view to improving airflow. Gandini also restyled the dashboard and the overall result was a pleasing and attractive car popularly referred to as Miura Spider. Following its introduction at the Brussels show, Sgarzi was pressed by buyers and dealers to accept orders. But Ferruccio stuck to his guns and refused to give the green light to the car for production, much to Sgarzi's disappointment. Part of this rationale was based on Bertone's wishes, because he liked to work in multiples of 50 units to enable him to spread the build cost, but Ferruccio was reluctant to commit to this number of roadsters.

The problem led, in effect, to Lamborghini branching into overseas production, and in a way that some Lamborghini purists did not like. The Miura Spider was sold to the International Lead Zinc Research Organization (ILZRO) in the USA. ILZRO supplied zinc, aluminium and other allows to the motor industry and wanted the car as part of its marketing programme.

The car, dismantled and rebuilt with parts plated in ILZRO's metals, was popularly called the Zn 75 and its dashing lines made it an ideal promotional vehicle. At the end of its promotional life, the Zn 75 was sold to the Boston Motor Museum in Massachusetts where it was exhibited until 1989 when David Jolliffe, the UK Lamborghini distributor, shipped it to Britain.

The car was exhibited at the Diablo launch in January 1990 at Monte Carlo where it won the Pirelli Trophy for the rarest Lamborghini on show. In 1990, the car was sold to a Lamborghini collector in Japan.

For Lamborghini, 1968 was a triumphant year and Ferruccio's other businesses were also expanding. Extra room for building cars was created at Sant'Agata with the addition of improved customer care facilities and more investment in plant and research and development. New models had been well received and the pre-sold order book was growing; 353 cars were delivered to buyers in that year.

There was though trouble ahead. In the early days, Ferruccio made full use of head-hunters to recruit his core team, and in the late 1960s he was on the receiving end.

CHAPTER 02

Giampaolo Dallara was contacted by advisers acting for De Tomaso (a Lamborghini rival) and left in August 1968 to make the short journey to Modena. From day one after joining Lamborghini in 1963, Dallara supervised the first revision of the Bizzarrini 350 GT engine. He had openly tried to convince Ferruccio to participate in motorsport to race-prove the marque but the founder never budged from his belief that it would be a costly mistake.

With group profits on the rise, Ferruccio could at this time probably have easily afforded to explore a race programme but even building prototypes was against his philosophy.

Ferruccio used to explain it like this: 'I wish to build GT cars without defects – quite normal, conventional but perfect – not a technical bomb,' and with Islero and Espada he had fulfilled this aim.

Full throttle: the Jarama GT *(top)* and Miura Roadsters, two models developed during a hectic period at Lamborghini in the late 1960s. Espada *(left)* was in production for ten years and 1217, were built.

How he came to square this with Miura is not totally clear though he maintained that in its road-going form, it did match his ambitions. So it was not a complete surprise that Dallara was persuaded to join De Tomaso, another entrepreneurial sports car manufacturer – and one with a Formula One project that Dallara, a gifted engineer, was recruited to head.

Unfortunately for Dallara, this F1 programme, like so many others, lacked the weight of funding to enable the enterprise to make any impression. The car manufacturer just managed to survive this experience but Dallara could see that De Tomaso lacked resources and he soon left the company.

Ferruccio, recognising the heavy demands on his engineering department, turned to Paulo Stanzani who had joined at the same time as Dallara, and was effectively his assistant. Stanzani was well qualified to assume Dallara's role and appointed technical director.

At the start of 1969, another problem loomed at Sant'Agata. When Ferruccio opened the factory, aided by generous tax breaks and other financial incentives from the Bolognese local authority, he had in return agreed that all employees would always be employed as full union members. In the late 1960s, Italian industry's relationship with its metal workers' union was fraught and for the first time Lamborghini – with the largest part of its workforce being metal machinists or fabricators – was disrupted by one-hour token stoppages as part of a national campaign.

Ferruccio, who had started the company because of his love of engineering, was never one to spend too much time in his own office or the boardroom. One of his strengths was as a motivator and he liked to mix with his staff on the factory floor. Because of this, he was soon made personally aware of a cooling of the atmosphere on his frequent visits to the assembly lines and other production areas. Even so, Lamborghini team spirit continued and, on a personal basis, both sides continued to respect each other.

During 1969, Lamborghini's management executed a thorough evaluation of the product range and the way the cars were built, an essential exercise as the manufacturer grew. The three models in production were revised and the Islero was upgraded to Islero S, with the engine developed to 350bhp. This was coupled with small changes to the styling so minor as to be hardly visible. The production version of the Miura S had an improved suspension and an increase in power to 375bhp at 7700rpm.

The most important change to the Espada was an increase in rear headroom, achieved by lowering the floor. The transmission and brakes were updated. Motoring writers have

CHAPTER 02

Radical action: the Miura SV (above and opposite with Lotus Elan), appeared at the 1971 Geneva motor show after substantial improvements to the original model.

given differing estimates of the Espada's top speed, but 150mph was achieved on a German autobahn over a measured flying kilometre.

During 1969 the team at the heart of the collaboration between Bertone and Lamborghini started work on a replacement for the Islero, which had hardly been a roaring success (only 100 were built during that year). The new model was to be named Jarama after an area of Spain famous for breeding fighting bulls, though Ferruccio was initially worried the name would be confused with the Jarama race track. The brief to Bertone was that the car should retain a four-seat configuration built on a shortened chassis but have greater performance than the Espada.

Lamborghini remained faithful to the 3929cc V12 but increased its compression ratio to 10.5/1. The chassis (construction was to be subcontracted out) would be shipped to Bertone to be combined with the body assembly, and then transported on to Sant'Agata for the fitting of all the Lamborghini components.

The Jarama 400 GT was seen first at the 1970 Geneva motor show when Paulo Stanzani was secretly at work on a radical new car that would use no parts from any previous Lamborghini. Following the investment in the plant, it was felt the factory had a capacity to manufacture up to 1,000 engines, transmissions and other major components each year.

The Lamborghini management was certain that sort of volume could not be achieved with the 3929cc V12 engine and all were aware of coming changes to Italy's tax laws that would penalise large engines. The directors were also concious of Ferrari's success with the 246 Dino, and Porsche's with the 911, and that led to the decision to build an all-new car based on a transverse 2.5-litre V8 engine.

Stanzani and Bertone/Gandini were pressured into developing the car inside nine months. Ferruccio's brief to Gandini was that the car also had to be a 2+2, which was Lamborghini's first concession to practicality – it acknowledged that people owning the car might have children.

This new product, known as P250, was to be named Urraco after another breed of fighting bull. Following two styling exercises, a third by Gandini gained the approval of Ferruccio. Stanzani had designed a new V8 engine with single overhead camshafts which on Sant'Agata testbeds produced a respectable 220bhp at 5000rpm. There was little time for bench running before body and engine were united at Sant'Agata in 1969 and road testing and development by Wallace started in earnest, with a deadline to present the car at the 1970 Turin motor show the following spring. The technical department was also under pressure to

adapt the current production models to new laws that were on the horizon in some export markets. The USA - always a very important market for Lamborghini - was probably the first country to recognise that car manufacturers had to be regulated in terms of safety and exhaust pollution. The Americans were certainly the first to move in to requiring testing and approval of impact bumpers and emission controls.

With Ferruccio pushing the development team, the car was ready for the Turin show where journalists enthused about the first small Lambo and its styling.

Given the 2+2 configuration, with transverse V8, the cockpit had to be moved well forward, leaving an unusually short front end and giving the car a distinctive profile. No delivery dates were quoted at the show as the factory knew that much development work was still required.

Meanwhile, Bob Wallace remained determined to get Lamborghini onto the race circuit. While development work continued on the Urraco, he devoted much of his own time in 1970 to extensively modifying a Miura S by completely rebuilding the suspension, reducing weight, extracting more power and adding spoilers to enhance road holding. Wallace saw the car as the perfect prototype for GT racing and it was designated the Miura S Jota. But his proposals for racing met with the inevitable 'no' from Ferruccio and, to his chagrin, Lamborghini sold the car to an Italian enthusiast to bring the project to a halt.

The Miura S Jota had a short life because the new owner wrote it off in an accident. The resulting publicity persuaded many Miura owners to attempt to modify their cars into replicas and the car had something approaching a cult following in Germany, though none of these replicas was able to produce the speed and handling of the Wallace Jota.

During 1970, Lamborghini undertook another immense project - the development programme for a possible replacement for the Miura, which did not totally conform to Ferruccio's overall brand philosophy. He accepted that while the car was radical, and to a large extent pioneering, he found the noise levels unacceptable. That had been one of his criticisms of Ferrari, and he was not minded to have the same accusation levelled at him.

The problem, he told his engineers, was caused by an extremely powerful engine mounted transversely just behind the driver's head. Ferruccio felt noise insulation was probably not possible and instructed Stanzani and his team to again collaborate with Bertone. Lamborghini engineers designed a new and longer chassis to accept the V12 engine to be mounted longitudinally.

This model was designated LP500 with the number indicating that Stanzani had

Badges of pride: the manufacturer's name in chrome on a Miura, and Ferruccio's beloved Fighting Bull emblem, as it was displayed at Lamborghini dealerships.

developed the 4-litre V12 to 5 litres by increasing the bore and stroke. Therefore, the engine grew from the normal 3929cc to 4971cc. There was another departure from company procedure because the chassis was designed and built in-house by Lamborghini to a tubular space frame configuration.

Legend has it that when Ferruccio was visiting Bertone to see the styling of the new LP500, an employee who was also taking a first look at the car was heard to exclaim: 'Countach!'. This was an earthy local dialect word with no literal translation into English but a polite equivalent might be 'fantastic!'.

As usual, an international motor show provided a deadline, and work was to proceed on the LP500/Countach at pace so the car would be ready for the Geneva motor show in spring 1971. Another big demand on engineering time was the Miura P400 SV, which also had to be ready for the same show. With knowledge gained in part from the Jota, the Miura SV was subjected to a radical revision, with improved handling through independent rear suspension, revision of the engine and transmission and a dry sump offered as a customer option.

The huge volume of work overstretched the research and development department and the team was unable to maintain the work schedule created for the Urraco and Countach, Lamborghini's two most important projects at that time. It was effectively two more years before either was ready for realistic delivery dates.

For Ferruccio, 1971 marked a turning point in the fortunes of his group. He came under mounting financial pressure for the first time as he sought to sustain the investment demands of his four manufacturing companies.

He was though cheered by the Geneva motor show which was arguably Lamborghini's most exciting, with five models on the stand: Miura SV, Espada 2, Urraco P250, Jarama GT and the LP500 Countach concept. Seven years after the 350 launched the company onto the car market, Lamborghini had definitely become of age, but difficulties lay ahead.

The whole group was to be buffeted by a world recession, soaring petrol prices, material shortages and industrial unrest. There was major trouble for Lamborghini Trattori which exported around 50 per cent of its production – Cento, the importer for South Africa, cancelled all its orders. Then, following a change of government, the new authorities in Bolivia dishonoured letters of credit for a large order of tractors that were at the docks in Genoa awaiting shipment or part-built at the factory. Italy and other countries cut back orders and the factory quickly found itself with hundreds of unwanted tractors.

CHAPTER 02

Ferruccio's agreement with the unions – which had been so attractive at the beginning – came back to bite him. It meant he was unable to cut costs on wages, and employees were paid whether they were actively engaged or idle. This rapidly produced a snowballing effect, especially with suppliers.

Despite having his back to the wall, and facing a desperate fight to save his company, Ferruccio felt no bitterness. He always believed the unions did a good job for the workers of Italy, and he never forgot his heritage as a son of the land.

But rumours began to spread and before long Lamborghini Automobili was sucked into an environment of suspicion that started to circulate about the group. Ferruccio reacted like the fighting bull that he was at heart, and towards the end of 1971 he drew all the cash he could extract from various accounts to go to the aid of his beloved automobile division by paying suppliers pressing the hardest.

His closest associates said later he offered to pay half the balance owed in cash, and if this was rejected he threatened to give the business to alternative suppliers. In battling to save his group, Ferruccio was helped by the good relations Lamborghini had cultivated, and it seems no supplier was prepared to take the company to court, with most accepting the cash offer.

Early 1972 brought no economic relief and the cash flow problems hindering the development of Countach and Urraco became protracted. The only new model at the 1972 Geneva motor show was the updated version of the Jarama P400 GTS.

Urraco development continued, with Stanzani experiencing reliability problems with the V8. As a cost-cutting exercise, the Countach reverted to an improved version of the original 4-litre engine, namely the V12 3929cc, but it was beefed up to 365bhp.

With neither of these two key new models ready to be put into production and attract orders with deposits, further strain was placed on Lamborghini's cash flow. Union problems rumbled on and it was hardly surprising that chairing four companies was taking its toll on Ferruccio. His son Tonino was reluctant to join either the tractor or the car business and the boss reluctantly accepted he must try to sell all or part of the two companies.

Ferruccio entered negotiations with Georges-Henri Rossetti, a car enthusiast from a wealthy Swiss family whose business interests included ownership of one of the country's leading watch and clock face manufacturers. Rossetti had bought an Islero and an Espada, and he and Ferruccio were friends which made the business negotiation easier though it must have been a bitter disappointment for Mr Lamborghini.

Money problems: the economic downturn forced Lamborghini to slow development of the Countach *(opposite)*.

CHAPTER 02

Countach! a Bertone employee, on seeing the car for the first time, uttered a local dialect word roughly equivalent to 'fantastic!'

Ferruccio was forced to face the unpalatable reality that the end was nigh. All his business guile failed to provide him with an escape route: he was wounded and facing the end.

With great sadness, Ferruccio accepted the need to relinquish total control of Automobili Lamborghini, by selling 51 per cent to Rossetti for what seemed at the time the miserly sum of about $600,000/£300,000.

That was bad enough, but Ferruccio then had to sell his entire holding in Lamborghini Tractors to an Italian group called S.A.M.E for an amount that has never been disclosed. S.A.M.E is now Italy's second largest tractor manufacturer after Fiat and still produces a vehicle branded Lamborghini, painted in Ferruccio's distinctive black and white colour scheme.

Ferruccio remained at Sant'Agata, running the car plant, though he now had only a minority stake. The relationship with Rossetti was always going to be difficult as the Swiss businessman was an absentee shareholder. He left the workload to Ferruccio who persevered with the development of Countach LP400 and the Urraco. Both cars reappeared at the 1973 Geneva show. The production programme reflected likely demand

"With great sadness, Ferruccio accepted the need to relinquish total control of Automobili Lamborghini, by selling 51 per cent to Rossetti"

for the cars, and dealers placed their orders.

Lamborghini's dealers were encouraged by the reception given to the new models at Geneva and Ferruccio displayed his customary confidence. Privately, though, he shared the same concern as Sgarzi the sales director and the dealer council – Lamborghini cars, with the exception of the Jarama GTS, did not match the build and reliability standards that had been Ferruccio's trademark.

Because of this, and the part time approach of a non-engineering Swiss major shareholder, Ferruccio was easily persuaded in 1974 to sell his remaining 49 per cent shareholding to another Swiss, Rene Leimer, for 600,000 Swiss francs (about $400,000/£200,000). Leimer, although a friend of Rossetti, had a different background, and was a self-made man whose wealth was derived from a business that laid underground electrical cable over long distances.

With his signature on a contract, Ferruccio severed his connection with his car factory and had already disposed of the tractor business. He did though retain ownership of Lamborghini Bruciatori, the air conditioning manufacturer, and of Lamborghini Oleodynamica Spa, which produced hydraulic valves (this was the last business he created and possibly the most profitable).

These two companies were managed by his son Tonino, and Ferruccio retired to La Fiorita, his estate near Perugia in Umbria, where he turned his mind to producing wine instead of cars and tractors. At the time he sold it, Lamborghini Automobili was unprofitable but the dividends Ferruccio received earlier had made him a relatively wealthy man.

Ferruccio's red wine was of good though not great quality. It was officially called Colli del Trasimeno but came to be known by a far more evocative and appropriate name – Sangue (blood) di Miura.

"The loyal employees were being asked to accept that their destiny was in the hands of foreigners who, many sensed, saw Lamborghini as just another money-making venture"

03_The challenger on its knees

Georges-Henri Rossetti and Rene Leimer, the two Swiss businessmen, became joint owners of Lamborghini in late 1973 with a lengthy list of problems to occupy their minds. They took an apartment in San Giovanni (about five miles away from the plant) so they could both devote enough time to their acquisition, and nurture it back to full health. That, at least, was the theory.

The question being asked at the time by motor industry professionals around the world was: are these the right men to have custody of a shaky Lamborghini?

For Rossetti and Leimer, the first task was to help the workforce adjust to life without Ferruccio: their boss was no longer the man who was the very essence of the factory and its cars. The loyal employees were being asked to accept that their destiny was in the hands of foreigners who, many sensed, saw Lamborghini as just another money-making venture. Early hostility was initially allayed by the enthusiasm of Leimer, but he and Rossetti were to be confronted later with the union action and other problems that had

On the right lines: the Countach LP400 was the only Lamborghini to conform to new safety tests in the 1970s.

CHAPTER 03

In the red: the inviting interior *(above)* **of an Espada, with the leather finished in a colour closely associated with Lamborghini's greatest rival.**

Under wraps: the Urraco prototype *(right)* **near the extension (still under construction) where it was to be built.**

forced Ferruccio into reluctant retirement.

In 1973, the workforce of more than 300 was focused on producing the established Espada and on marketing activity to try to increase sales of the Jarama 400 GTS. When production of the Miura SV had finished at the end of 1972, Stanzani and his engineering team were under pressure to ensure development took the Countach LP500 and the P250 Urraco into production as quickly as possible. Stanzani's design of the 5-litre engine intended for the Countach was such a radical reworking that the time and the cost involved was too great, Rossetti and Leimer decided, and they reverted to the faithful 3929cc V12 that had powered previous Lamborghinis.

Even so, many alterations were needed to make possible the driving characteristics and performance essential to the Countach, and Wallace led the extensive testing of the prototype, by now called the Countach LP400 (for it was to have a 4- and not 5-litre engine). Weighing only 1065kg, it could easily exceed the magical 300kph (186mph) and accelerate to 100kph (62mph) in just over five seconds, making it officially the fastest road car on the market. Ferruccio must have approved of that.

At the end of two and a half years of development, the P250 Urraco at last went into production at the end of 1973 following its appearance at the Geneva motor show. In 1974, only 30 or so Urracos went to customers, proving that venturing into a difficult market sector with a small car was a big gamble. The manufacturing costs were based on building a minimum of 500 units a year to break even and belief in the reality of this ambitious figure stemmed from the confidence of the American dealer network that it alone could sustain sales at this level.

There was though a fundamental flaw in the equation, for the US dealers' assessment was born out of earlier data and commercial information from Lamborghini, which included the promise that the car resembled a small Miura. In reality, the Urraco was not what they expected to be asked to sell, and failing to stop this muddle exposed a lack of experience in the automotive sector that was beginning to put the two Swiss owners in financial danger.

Then came another setback. Lamborghini had to go to the expense of putting the P250 Urraco through US type approval tests to prove that it was safe and conformed with exhaust pollution, noise and other regulations. With the benefit of hindsight, it was a waste of money.

In Europe the outlook was more cheerful. The motoring press praised the Urraco's handling and most journalists who drove the car liked the 2+2 seating format, though there was criticism of the suede dashboard and driving position. Performance was considered to be no more than adequate for a car in this sector.

The Urraco was to run into more serious trouble when the engine failed to meet the challenges set by hard-driving, high-mileage owners. Some found that the rubber camshaft drive-belt broke, which caused damaged cylinder heads, bent valves and other mechanical problems.

Sales of the Urraco in 1974 were dented by the arrival of the Ferrari 308 GTB, the Maranello company's response to the challenge from Lamborghini. Its looks were of universal appeal and it was quicker than its Lamborghini rival.

Rossetti and Leimer had inherited the extension to the Sant'Agata plant which Ferruccio wanted for the assembly of the Urraco, but over its five-year life only 520 were built, and the model was a major disappointment. Espada and Jarama sales were near enough budget but Lamborghini was failing to achieve production at the level demanded by overall costs.

CHAPTER 03

The Countach looked as though it could be a winner but required more development to reach the build quality demanded by purchasers.

Lamborghini thought at one time that an increase in power might set sales of the Urraco ablaze. At the 1974 Turin motor show, the model was relaunched with the V8 90-degree engine uprated to 2996cc and developing 250bhp at 7500rpm. To remedy the failings of the 2.5-litre engine, Lamborghini added dual-change camshafts and a five-bearing crankshaft. The engine was now strong, and performance rivalled that of competitors, but the car looked the same and retained the Urraco name. It was tainted by the disappointment caused by the earlier P250, and sales were to prove poor.

Rosetti and Leimer also took a gamble on another less powerful and cheaper model. They hoped to take advantage of high taxation levels placed on cars with engines of more than two litres in Italy following the Middle East oil crisis and petrol shortages. They believed Italians would buy a 2-litre Urraco and the P200 went on sale with the Urraco 250 bodyshell, powered by a 1973cc, single overhead camshaft producing 182bhp at 7500rpm. The car had a claimed top speed of 132mph but Italians did not take to it, and only 66 were sold over the three years it was on sale.

The Countach LP400, seen first at the 1974 Geneva show, created some much needed optimism with the launch of what many regard as the greatest Lamborghini. In the same year came the arrival of the Bertone Bravo, which was penned by Gandini and built on the chassis and floorpan of the 3-litre Urraco, known as the P300. The styling was brilliant but much soul searching was needed to work out how the car could be developed for production.

Even at this early stage, Rossetti and Leimer were experiencing difficulties with the factory's funding and cash flow. Leimer said later that Lamborghini suffered as a business because the level of credit enjoyed by Ferruccio from his suppliers was cut for the new owners. Less money was available for research and development and under-capitalisation always stalked their ownership. Successful new models were needed as the factory's capacity had been enlarged to produce power and transmission units, and to assemble up to 1,000 cars a year.

Bertone was astute enough to recognise the value of the Lamborghini brand name and wanted to exploit the commercial potential of his association with the manufacturer. So he agreed to design and build the Bravo at his own expense. He retained ownership of the car but Bravo was destined to progress no further than a design and concept car, displayed at various motor shows on either the Lamborghini or Bertone stand. Dealers from around the

In the lead: a Lamborghini Countach LP500S edges ahead of a Ferrari Testarossa in an independent test.

Open and shut: two views of the Countach LP400, which generated some much needed optimism at a time when morale was low at Lamborghini.

> "Rossetti and Leimer wanted to put the necessary money into developing the Bravo for production but were restricted by their existing business commitments"

world, and the thousands of other visitors to the shows, were enthusiastic about the Bravo and no wonder: its lines were a joy.

Rossetti and Leimer wanted to put the necessary money into developing the Bravo for production but were restricted by their existing business commitments. After two years of promotional work, the project was pensioned off to the Bertone motor museum. It had turned out to be yet another costly mistake.

There were continuing problems with the production models in 1975. Only around 100 Countach were completed because construction time was so lengthy. The space frame chassis was contracted out, with the aluminium body cladding hand made and fabricated at Sant'Agata. This method of production was slow and failed to meet demand from the dealer network, which meant that the waiting list started to grow. Meanwhile, Espada 3 and Jarama GTS were built to order.

Urraco continued in 1975, though the P250 (first drawn in 1959) had been phased out in Europe in 1974 and was to continue in the US only until 1976.

The 3-litre engine of the Urraco P300 has been described as a 'jewel' but sales were much lower than expected. In part this was due to the reluctance of Rossetti and Leimer to order bodyshells from Bertone in sufficient numbers to spread the manufacturer's engineering costs.

Given a firm order for 1,000 bodyshells, Bertone could have quoted a much lower price for each unit. As it was, Bertone was forced to quote a much higher price-per-unit for a dribble of orders, as it needed to at least recover its design and initial production costs as quickly as possible.

Rosetti and Leimer lacked the cash reserves to commit themselves, and right-hand drive Urracos were in reality built to order, though customers were never told.

To ease their cash flow worries, the two owners liked to see pre-sold vehicles moving down the production line but this cautious approach meant dealers were forced to quote a long delivery date and too many potential buyers went elsewhere.

In another attempt to save the Urraco, Leimer looked again at a prototype developed earlier by Wallace and his associates and based on the third Bertone P250 bodyshell, referred to in the factory as the Urraco Rally. Wallace had modified the engine, tweaked the suspension and added bodywork improvements including spoilers.

The changes were slightly reminiscent of his work on the Jota, the name given to the racing version of the Miura, which he worked on mainly in his own time.

CHAPTER 03

Leimer asked Bertone to restyle a P300 by combining a targa top (lift-out panels) and Wallace's revised mechanical advances. The car was named Silhouette and the Swiss owners somehow found the money to build the car and finance a marketing strategy to position it away from the Urraco.

The Silhouette performed and handled well, and the model deserved better success than the 55 sales it achieved Lamborghini's reluctance to finance certification for the US market was a major factor in the car's failure. Sgarzi, the sales supremo, always felt that introducing the Silhouette to the American market would have ensured its success,

The biggest problem for Lamborghini in 1975 was the loss to the engineering department of both Stanzani, the head of engineering, and Wallace, who had been so influential in pre-production development.

Stanzani was in part feeling the burden of the failure of the P250 and believed that Leimer's demands on the development department were excessive. Wallace felt his role with the Countach was essentially done and, with no new supercar project on the

Uphill struggle: the Espada *(right)*, one of four Lamborghini models that failed to meet new safety-related regulations without a costly major redesign.

Performance block: a planned five-litre engine was shelved and the Countach 500S used a 4754cc unit *(above right)*.

Lamborghini horizon, left to pursue his interest in competition cars.

He joined the team looking after Harrah's Automobile Collection in the US. Bill Harrah made a fortune from casinos and in 1946 bought and restored a 1911 Maxwell, going on to build a collection of 1,400 cars, and some were displayed in a museum that opened to visitors in 1962.

Lamborghini's ability to attract good engineers continued with the arrival of Franco Baraldini and Luigi Campelini from Ferrari to head the engineering department. The company's problem was that their arrival coincided with the two Swiss owners starting to fall out. Rossetti was becoming more and more of a recluse and rarely went to the factory, preferring to have evening business meetings at his apartment. Rossetti's odd behaviour caused many bizarre and unpleasant ill-founded rumours to sweep around the factory. The truth is that Rossetti suffered from a psychological condition that made him afraid to go out in daylight.

Leimer was striving to do his best for Lamborghini but the company's finances had never been properly secure from day one. He was in a difficult position as he was spending much of his time struggling with the finances rather than the product and, in addition, was also neglecting his core business (laying underground cable) in Switzerland. A further pressure was his lack of experience in the auto business, and Leimer was ill-equipped to deal with the constant disputes and walk-outs orchestrated by the unions which affected businesses throughout Italy in the 1970s.

As the day-to-day problems mounted, Lamborghini faced a major decision. New European Union legislation meant that cars to be sold from 1978 would require a national type approval certificate. These rules meant that every component in every car manufacturer's model range would have to be certified as meeting safety regulations which were far stricter than anything Lamborghini had previously experienced for certification in the USA. On top of that, America was in the process of making its tests even more rigorous.

Type approval, also known within the motor industry as homologation, is a very costly and protracted exercise. It starts with the destruction of a vehicle which is subjected to impacts to the front, rear and side. The manufacturer needs to demonstrate that the car's strength and energy-absorbing crumple zones are sufficiently well designed to protect driver and passengers to the point specified in the regulations.

Every part of the car's construction has to be detailed in a matrix and the car stripped and inspected by the relevant government agency. To do this, car manufacturers set up a new department devoted to type approval and an appraisal is carried out to check whether existing production models would be able to pass these tests.

For Lamborghini, the result of that assessment brought devastating news because, without major redesign, Espada, Jarama, Urraco and Silhouette would all fail to get type approval. Only the Countach LP400, with its space frame chassis, would meet the safety test. Lamborghini faced up to the inevitable and accepted that once type approval came into play, it would be left with only one model – an uprated Countach designated the 400S, which was exhibited at the 1978 Geneva show.

Britain's Motor Industry Research Agency (MIRA) was one of the few centres whose crash test results were recognised throughout Europe, though the UK in the 1970s did not recognise tests carried out in other European countries.

Only Countach needed to be taken to MIRA for type approval tests because the other models were to cease production by early 1978 when the new regulations came into effect.

Lamborghini continued to try to make improvements in an effort to increase sales. The Espada was offered with a Chrysler automatic gearbox, though this was not a happy union as the lack of development time meant that at 10mph the 1,000 revs were not enough to operate the brake servo. Hardly surprisingly, the car was not well received and this was a further blow to Lamborghini's standing when it was already in decline.

The 400S evolved with wider track and wheel arches, revised suspension and a front spoiler. The distinctive rear wing, which most customers wanted, would not have passed the national type approval regulations and so had to be fitted as an aftersale option.

Lamborghini, in its sales literature, offered to fit the wings at first service, though in reality this happened to suit the owner. The interior of the 400S was redesigned and, when announced in 1978, the car was praised by both the motoring press and Lamborghini buyers.

Behind the scenes, two events were unfolding in 1977 and 1978 that were to crucially affect the future of the company. Lamborghini desperately sought collaboration with other manufacturers to sustain the engineering capabilities that existed at the factory and two projects arrived at almost the same time.

Luigi Campelini, Lamborghini's senior engineer, introduced BMW to the factory and secured an agreement that Sant'Agata would develop a new car for the German manufacturer, designated the M1. BMW has since retained the M series as a title indicating a top-of-the-range, high-performance model. Four prototypes were commissioned by BMW using Lamborghini's knowledge of rear-engine layouts and Campelini, in collaboration with the independent stylist Giugiaro, worked on the shape of the car.

BMW approved the vehicle and entered into a production agreement that Lamborghini would build up to 400 of the cars at Sant'Agata. Part of the deal specified that BMW would supply components on credit and also prepay for parts acquired by Lamborghini from outside suppliers. This was a highly attractive contract for Lamborghini and helped to solve Leimer's chronic cash flow dilemma.

The second turned out to be something of a poisoned chalice. The project was based on a vehicle known as the Cheetah. It came from Mobility Technology International (MTI), an American company seeking a prestige car manufacturer to develop an off-road vehicle capable of rapid speeds across all terrains. The vehicle was seen to have a potential military application but the project was fated from the start.

Things started well enough, with Lamborghini securing a loan from the Italian government to offset part of the development cost of both the BMW M1 and the Cheetah, but MTI was unable to contribute financially. The company was bogged down in copyright disputes in the USA over allegations that the vehicle was a copy of the Ford Motor Company's XR311.

CHAPTER 03

Speed test: a Lamborghini Countach takes on a motorcycle for a picture sequence set up by a motoring magazine.

When the Cheetah was exhibited in 1977 at Lamborghini's spiritual home (the Geneva show), there were serious threats of legal action from Ford against MTI. The Cheetah, equipped with a 5.9-litre Chrysler engine matched to an auto transmission, was displayed as a Lamborghini.

Potential customers and the motoring press were left confused as to why Lamborghini would want to get involved with a vehicle aimed at a totally alien market place for an Italian supercar maker, namely the military.

Inevitably, the vehicle was a long way off being ready for appraisal or production and the unit cost of each vehicle would have to reflect the high additional costs of the use of Lamborghini engines and transmissions. Lamborghini's cash flow could not sustain the tooling needed for the BMW project and the development of the Cheetah. The company was behind schedule with production of the M1 and paid the ultimate price – BMW lost confidence and cancelled the project, moving it to Baur of Germany. The M1 was to have been built on production line one (vacant since the axing of the Espada) and which was to remain empty for 12 months.

This left Lamborghini, in 1978, with only the Countach 400S to sell and a cash-guzzling Cheetah in the development shop. At his home in Switzerland that year, Leimer admitted to business visitors (including his UK importer) that the position was grave.

The reality was that Leimer was struggling alone for Lamborghini because his partner Rossetti was making no contribution from his Swiss company. Lamborghini was so starved of money that it lacked even the resources to increase production of the 400S, and Leimer was desperately trying to attract new projects and investors.

He was close at that time to attracting Walter Woolf, a wealthy Lamborghini enthusiast who employed hundreds of

divers, and had contracts to maintain dozens of offshore oil rigs. Woolf decided in the end that he would drive Lamborghinis but not risk an investment in the manufacturer.

Leimer did though raise a loan, secured on the factory, from a US businessman, Zoltan Reti, who was soon to be disillusioned by Lamborghini as an investment and took action that might have felled the Fighting Bull.

In late 1978, Reti successfully applied to the Court of Bologna for AFL Spa to be declared bankrupt, and the court appointed Dr Alexandro Artese as the receiver. Artese was an accountant and, by good fortune, also a car enthusiast. It was clear from the first creditors' meeting that he intended to try to save the factory rather than wind it up.

His first appointment was to recruit Guilio Alfieri, an experienced engineer whose successes at Maserati both as a designer and administrator were well known in the industry. The efforts of Artese and Alfieri ensured that key people at the plant were retained, and with goodwill from Lamborghini's dealers and customers, production of the Countach 400S was maintained through 1979 and 1980, ensuring the survival of the Lamborghini brand.

At this point, the Mimran family came onto the scene with two brothers, Patrick and Jean-Claude, closely monitoring events at Lamborghini throughout 1980. The Mimran family had substantial business interests including flour and mining industries in East Africa and when, in early 1981, Artese decided to bring discussions to a conclusion, the Mimran brothers were the only interested party with the resources to make a deal.

Their bid of $3m/£1.25m for the assets of AFL Spa was successful and the Mimran brothers registered a new company – Nuova Automobili Ferruccio Lamborghini Spa. Patrick, aged 24, was appointed president of Lamborghini, with his elder brother Jean-Claude (35) supporting him.

During the receivership, Artese and Alfieri had worked tirelessly to keep the factory alive and protect jobs. Employees were especially indebted to Alfieri who, from time to time, paid wages at the factory out of his own bank account. Through his efforts, there was also occasional financial support from two Lamborghini dealerships, Achilli Motors of Milan, and Emilianauto of Bolgna.

Alfieri was a talented engineer and, in addition to his administrative duties, ensured the development and the production of the Countach 400S. Alfieri also used this period to develop a replacement for the P300 Urraco and the Silhouette.

This new model, destined to continue the tradition of Ferruccio, was named after

> "Rossetti and Leimer must have felt like victims of some form of Lamborghini curse, but the owners who followed them showed what could be done with business skill and adequate financial resources"

another fighting bull, the Jalpa. Bertone gave some assistance but the car was primarily developed at the factory, and completed in time to debut at the 1981 Geneva motor show.

The Rossetti/Leimer ownership of the factory e ended with the appointment of the receiver and they were left as unsecured creditors, returning to Switzerland. They were to receive nothing from the sale by Artese to the Mimrans because secured creditors took preference.

Rossetti, dogged by ill-health for many years, is believed to have lost his family business and in early 2004 was living frugally. Leimer became so desperate in his attempts to save his Swiss business that he turned to crime. He was involved with a ring of people dealing in stolen luxury cars, arrested, charged and spent three years in prison in Switzerland in the early 1990s. He died in 2002, aged 62.

Rossetti and Leimer must have felt like victims of some form of Lamborghini curse, but the owners who followed them showed what could be done with business skill and adequate financial resources. The Mimrans were to show there was money to be made from the business at Sant'Agata building rarified supercars.

"Their achievement was all the more remarkable because they took over at a time when the Lamborghini brand name had lost much of its shine"

04_Frenchmen mount a rescue

Patrick and Jean-Claude Mimran, the Frenchmen who were owners of Lamborghini between 1980 and 1987, achieved success after acquiring a business that was in receivership. Their achievement was all the more remarkable because they took over at a time when the Lamborghini brand name had lost much of its shine.

The man to be in control, as president of Lamborghini, was Patrick Mimran, a cosmopolitan living in Geneva. Though aged only 24, he was married with a family and had adopted the lifestyle of an international sophisticate: this was a man who would be at one with Lamborghini owners.

Patrick was already an avid collector of modern art, and so interested in popular music that he had a recording studio built at his home. He composed music in the style of Vangelis and launched a record label, with offices in London.

On February 29, 1980, the Mimran brothers entered into an agreement with the Bologna bankruptcy court to lease the company from its administration on a day to day basis.

In its element: a Countach 500S, with the driver relishing the open road ahead, and the chance to exploit the car's 375bhp when extended at 7000rpm.

Racing certainty: Luigi Marmaroli *(above)*, recruited by the Mimrans because of his motor sport experience to work on Countach and other projects.

Facing the challenge: Emile Novaro*(right)*, trusted by the Mimrans, was chosen to re-ignite Lamborghini and make it competitive with Ferrari and Maserati.

The court set 29 May 1981 as the deadline for a final bid for any purchasers and so Lamborghini entered a phase that seemed to represent more a temporary lifeline than its lasting salvation. In fact, the arrangement worked surprisingly well and confidence in the Mimrans' abilities soon rose among the workforce, suppliers, dealers and customers. The brothers ensured that both production and development continued while they carefully appraised Lamborghini and the investment required to bring the factory back to profitability – the company had been making a loss since 1972.

Patrick and Jean-Claude attracted little attention during their time at Lamborghini, which was probably because they got on with the job quietly and effectively. Against the odds, they re-established Lamborghini as a successful and desirable supercar manufacturer and Patrick spent a lot of time at the factory. He provided the money to finance an increase in production of the Countach while tackling a business plan embracing investment for new models and, ultimately, the long-term success of the factory.

A nucleus of experienced and enthusiastic engineers and technical staff at Lamborghini was keen to remain with the factory but the total labour force was down to around 160 people. Ubaldo Sgarzi met the Mimrans and he and they agreed it was a good idea for Lamborghini to retain the services of the man who had directed Lamborghini sales from day one.

The brothers also saw the need to make appointments from outside, and they managed to attract a long-standing and respected colleague from the Mimran family business. Emile Novaro, appointed Lamborghini's managing director, lived in Monte Carlo but the challenge of getting Lamborghini back into shape appealed to him.

Novaro's appointment was crucial because Sant'Agata desperately needed someone with drive and commercial realism to take responsibility for implementing the renaissance of the factory. Novaro was able to re-ignite the enthusiasm of the staff and the distributor network and foster a belief that under the Mimran stewardship Lamborghini would grow and eventually compete with Ferrari and Maserati. That had been Ferruccio's ambition and there were grounds for believing it could now become a reality.

In the early 1980s, the fortunes of Maserati were in decline at the Modena factory. Its only car worthy of the Maserati heritage was the Quadroporte, a large saloon that was not selling as well as expected. The board wanted to relaunch Maserati to try to re-establish the brand in a new market sector with the bi-turbo series. Giulio Alfieri was appointed general manager but continued with his existing responsibilities as head of design and engineering. It was a lot to ask of anyone.

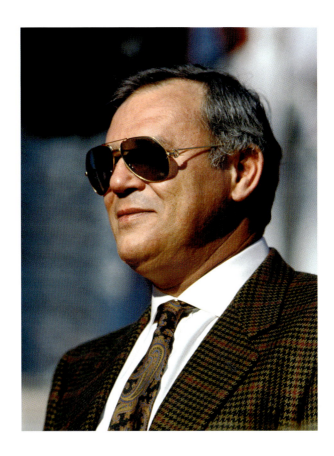

Lamborghini was facing challenges as the Mimrans took over. Its future success depended firstly on re-establishing the marque to a motoring public made sceptical by the slide in the value of used Lamborghinis, caused by the company going into receivership. Lower residual values inevitably dissuaded some would-be purchasers who were thinking about buying a new Lamborghini.

The Mimrans were experienced enough in business to realise that something had to be done quickly to demonstrate that Lamborghini was back in gear, and some smart marketing was also essential to stimulate demand for the product. The link with Bertone, perceptively forged by Ferruccio, still existed and it was agreed that Bertone produce a styling exercise: this was an open car named the Athon.

The car was not seriously considered to be a prototype that would lead to production but more a design exercise. Aggressively styled, it was certain to create interest.

The Mimrans decided to exhibit the Athon and the Countach 400S at the 1980 Turin motor show to demonstrate that Lamborghini was back in business. At the show, a press release stated that Countach 400S production was to be increased to fulfil outstanding orders and this optimistic news – combined with positive press coverage gained by the open-top Athon – combined to go a long way towards restoring faith in the Fighting Bull. The Athon never went into production but still creates interest among Lamborghini enthusiasts.

The creative energy of the factory's technical department continued to be focussed on the development of the new P350 Jalpa and the off-road LM, the vehicle that began life as the Cheetah, the inspiration of an American company.

Jalpa was chosen to continue the Lamborghini tradition of naming cars after breeds of fighting bulls, or areas where they came from. The car's styling was the result of a collaboration between Bertone and Lamborghini's Gandini and the Urraco V8 engine was developed to 3480cc, developing 255bhp at 7000rpm. The car leapt the type approval test hurdle and was launched at the 1981 Geneva motor show, with the factory ready to start deliveries in the same year.

Giulio Alfieri had produced a small Lamborghini with good all-round driving characteristics and it was an ancestor of the Gallardo, the second car to be completed during the reign of Audi.

The Jalpa was given a reasonably warm reception by the motoring press, and the build quality was good, but the car never achieved the forecast level of production.

Meanwhile, Novaro had the support of the Mimran brothers and was keen to push

CHAPTER 04

Rough road: the LM002 (above and opposite) struggled to find private owners and failed to convince the military that it was worth buying.

ahead with the development of the Cheetah, now code-named LM001, but the project failed to gain unanimous support among the senior team at Lamborghini. Ubaldo Sgarzi and others were far from confident that the off-road vehicle could achieve its intended sales volumes.

They were also sceptical about the wisdom of putting such a large proportion of the factory's manpower resources into a vehicle that was such a drastic departure from an image Lamborghini had taken 20 years to develop. With good reason, there were serious doubts about whether a rugged looking 4x4 was a logical model to be developed by a small Italian company producing exotic sports cars.

Despite all the misgivings, the new owners of the business decided to press ahead and authorised a full development programme to put the car into production.

The first model, the LM001, was rear-engined and initially used an eight-cylinder, 5900cc AMC engine imported from the USA, though that was soon to be replaced by Lamborghini's new V12 4754cc 60-degree engine. This power unit was also intended for use in an updated version of the Countach.

The development programme that started with the LM001 in 1981 continued until the definitive version, the LM002, went into production in 1986 (at the time, the longest gestation period for a Lamborghini). It was curious that the Mimrans, Novaro and Alfieri were convinced the military would be attracted by the vehicle's ability to do 100mph across sand. The project was so off the mark that the LM002 was never even given a name as a military vehicle.

Failure to think the project through properly from the start was illustrated by the decision in 1982 to move the engine from the rear to the front. It is unlikely that any car has survived such a rapid and fundamental change in design.

The main objective was to improve steering and handling, and also to enable some extra optional armament to be mounted at the rear. The LMA002, produced only with Lamborghini's V12 engine, was extensively tested in Europe and Africa.

The definitive version, the LM002 (note the removal of the letter 'A'), was evolved from this model and type approval was obtained for Europe and the USA leading up to its launch at the 1986 Geneva motor show.

While the top management at Lamborghini remained confident about the prospects of sales to armed forces around the world, not all distributors were convinced there would be demand in the public sector for an off-roader with a price tag of $110,000/£75,000. The

CHAPTER 04

Pace setter: the 455bhp engine (opposite) was powerful enough to keep the Countach Quattrovalvole at the top of the supercar league in terms of performance.

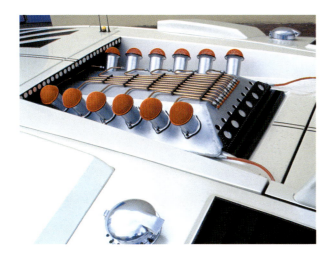

engine powering the car had evolved as Lamborghini's 5.2-litre quattro-valve version.

The LM002 was a highly technical vehicle with optional four-wheel drive and exceptional off-road speed. An obvious drawback was that the sophistication of the specification required high-quality technicians to maintain the vehicle, and expensive replacement parts would make it very difficult to secure any meaningful orders from the military. It lacked the fundamentals that had made the Jeep such a useful vehicle in World War II.

The LM002 was also likely to appeal – as some sort of glorified beach buggy – only to the wealthiest and most eccentric admirers of 4x4s.

Some journalists loved writing about it. Brock Yates (presumably with tongue in cheek) wrote in the October 1987 issue of America's influential Car & Driver magazine: 'When you order your LM002, consider the following modifications ... we recommend tinted glass. And more headlamps. And lots of antennas. Complete armor would be a good idea, though it would reduce the vehicle's performance. But a gunrack would be essential. For your Uzis, of course. See you soon on Rodeo Drive. Or in the center of Beirut. On the Khyber Pass. It's up to you."

The LM002 was burdened with serious flaws. Its power-to-weight ratio made the car a gas guzzler – a large fuel tank was essential because it returned a petrol consumption figure of only around 5mpg when driven hard. Another problem to dog the LM002 throughout its production life was the potentially dangerous and annoying smell of petrol that invaded the cabin (hardly something to be tolerated by people paying so much to buy one).

Misgivings about the chances of selling the vehicle in any useful numbers mounted, with some dealers reluctant to commit to placing orders. In the end, Lamborghini called its distributors to a meeting at the factory and it was agreed to allow each to decide whether or not to commit to orders (a rare state of affairs in the automotive business). The LM002 was never sold in the UK where it was viewed as a potential sales disaster.

In America, its prospects were more upbeat and Joe Nastase, then Lamborghini's East Coast importer based in New Jersey, supported its sale. Nastase worked closely with the factory because he obtained US certification for Lamborghinis in the USA. To do so for the LM002 was no mean achievement, as the US laws were at that time probably the most stringent of any country.

Lamborghini's confidence in the LM002 led to a deal with a Spanish coach builder, to supply the tubular-frame chassis and pre-painted bodyshell. Under the Initial contract, Lamborghini was committed to purchasing 500 painted bodyshells. Chrysler, when it later

CHAPTER 04

became the owner of Lamborghini, renegotiated the order down to 300.

Production of the LM002 and other projects all formed part of the Mimran business plan. Lamborghini was growing in stature and the economic climate following the recession of the 1970s was recovering.

Novaro recruited more highly qualified engineers to the Sant'Agata team. Massimo Ceccarani joined to supervise the technical development of production necessary for the successful passage through type approval. He remained committed to Lamborghini and became technical director under the Audi stewardship.

Luigi Marmaroli, an engineer with a motor racing background, joined the factory with responsibility to Alfieri for the development of Countach and special projects. The future of the engineering department was further underwritten by the Mimrans' financial strength and enthusiasm to expand the factory.

The Countach 400S was upgraded to 500S specification (4754cc engine, top speed of 186mph/300km/h – an increase of 9mph/15km/h, while power output was restored to 375bhp, a rise of 25bhp.

The Countach 500S looked identical to the 400S which continued to earn the admiration of the press and public alike. The 500S claimed the title of 'world's fastest road car' and following its debut at the 1982 Geneva motor show, the order book for this Lamborghini was full. Improvements to the production line enabled the company to build more than 100 of them in 1982.

Work continued on the Countach, with Marmaroli concentrating on the engine. The definitive version of that engine was announced in 1985 and designated the Quattrovalvole, following the reworking of the cylinder heads with four valves per cylinder. The cubic capacity was increased to 5167cc, with a power output of 455bhp at 7000rpm. This version of the Countach was fast enough to keep Lamborghini at the top of the supercar league in terms of performance.

Under the management of the Mimrans, Lamborghini entered a settled time in the mid-1980s. Sales were meeting targets and research and development made good progress to ensure replacement models were ready in time. Sales of Lamborghini parts were also rising as the total number of its cars on roads around the world continued to rise, and the customer service department reported a steady upturn in revenues. Lamborghini had at last returned to viability.

Visiting Sant'Agata once again became a pleasure because the old enthusiasm that

Under achiever: the P350 Jalpa met with approval from the motoring press but failed to achieve the production figures that were forecast for it.

Ferruccio generated in the early days had returned to all who worked there. This air of confidence encouraged the management to arrange visits by dealers, suppliers and other business associates. Motoring journalists were invited and invariably wrote positive articles, which helped to enhance the reputation and image of Lamborghini and its cars to potential buyers around the world.

The LM002 off-roader was probably the biggest stride Lamborghini ever attempted to make (though in the wrong direction). A second project that evolved in the 1980s also marked a departure from its previous philosophy – the development of a 7-litre, V12 marine engine as an alternative power unit for the planned but ill-fated military version of the LM002. The Mimrans gave the go-ahead for the engine though never used for its military application, it was offered as an alternative power unit for US buyers of the LM002.

CHAPTER 04

The tops: a Jalpa 350, adapted to special order for a customer, with modifications including a prominent rear spoiler.

CHAPTER 04

Patrick Mimran and Emile Novaro were powerboat enthusiasts and keen to see whether the engine could be adapted for marine racing. Coincidentally, Danielle Audetto approached the factory in his capacity of team manager for Renato della Valle, a leading Class One (C1) offshore powerboat racer. C1 has since been renamed F1, in line with its motor racing equivalent.

Audetto was on the committee of UMI, the organisation responsible for running offshore powerboat racing. He was convinced that a petrol engine of less than 8.2 litres (the permitted maximum size) could beat diesel-engined craft, which at that time were dominant.

A deal was struck between Count Renato Della Valle and Lamborghini, in part financed by Cinzano and other sponsors, with Audetto taking a key role in bringing about a successful conclusion. Lamborghini designed a racing version of the L800 marine engine (8172cc, four valves per cylinder and a power output of more than 700 bhp).

Della Valle was to race his monohull twin-engined boat with factory support that included the time of engineers Seb Gallerani and Dominico Gaglioti.

Some success in 1982 - Della Valle was second in the round Britain powerboat race - led to requests from competing teams to purchase the engines, which cost around $85,000/£50,000 each.

Novaro was sufficiently confident in the project to set up a separate marine division at the factory and this has since grown year-on-year. It became such an important part of the factory's activities that, at times, it generated close to 10 per cent of total turnover. Audi, now the owner of Lamborghini, continued with the development of the marine engine department and in 2003 opened a new and larger self-contained division at the plant.

This is part of the Mimrans' continuing legacy. Their decision to back a brave venture has meant that for more than 20 years, Lamborghini has been the dominant force in offshore powerboat racing. First, the engine powered craft to victory in the European championships, and since then Lamborghini engines have brought triumph for teams in the world championships.

Steve Curtis, from Southampton, England, who started powerboat racing in 1985 has won more races for teams powered by Lamborghini engines than any other pilot, including the 2003 world championship.

Following the retirement of Della Valle from powerboat racing in 1985, Danielle Audetto was invited by Novaro to join Lamborghini as director of public relations and sports activities.

"Patrick Mimran and Emile Novaro were sensing success on the track, but needed to consider the investment"

Audetto, a former rally works driver for Lancia, and F1 team manager for Ferrari, was keen to see Lamborghini in sports endurance racing, with Le Mans as the prime objective.

Ferruccio fought many battles to stop Lamborghini entering motorsport but it was now back on the agenda, and this time with the support of Emile Novaro, who ran the company for the Mimran brothers.

Marmaroli had developed a 5.7-litre version of the Countach Quattrovalvole engine that was perfect for the rules running endurance racing in 1986. Technology in racing car chassis design was more advanced in the UK than in most parts of the world and Spice Engineering was commissioned to design and build a car to accommodate the Lamborghini 5.7-litre engine. Spice was based at Silverstone, the UK's F1 circuit.

Novaro and Audetto wanted to compete in the 1987 endurance racing series, and try for the big prize of success at the Le Mans 24-hour race. Sponsorship came from Unipart, which was promoting Supreme, its synthetic oil, in a deal brokered by David Jolliffe.

At that time, Spice Engineering was dominant in class 2 endurance racing (up to 3-litre – class 1 – was above that size), and had twice won its class at Le Mans. Portman, the UK Lamborghini importer, was responsible for the chassis and running the team in partnership with Marmaroli and Lamborghini provided engineers and engines. The car was completed in 1986 and testing and further development began to assess whether it was capable of challenging teams from Porsche and the other most successful manufacturers.

By the time testing was complete, only one race remained in the 1986 championship – the South African round at Kylami. Patrick Mimran gave the go-ahead for the car to race, subject to a final test session at Monza where, he said, the Lamborghini needed to achieve a lap time within one second of the winning Jaguar's fastest at the opening round of the championship at the circuit in April.

With so much at stake, there was tension in the air, deepened by an initial scare caused by the late arrival of the Dunlop support vehicle with race tyres. It was late afternoon when Mario Baldi, a former F1 test driver, took the Lamborghini out onto the circuit and equalled the lap record. This was the first step towards success and achieving the goal set by Patrick Mimran and sent a buzz of excitement through everyone associated with Lamborghini.

Competing in motor sport (let alone winning) demands finance and good business planning. Patrick Mimran and Emile Novaro were sensing success on the track, but needed to consider the investment. They sanctioned an investment for the first phase of the racing programme, and gave the project the green light. The car was taken to Kylami and,

Bright ideas: a detail *(opposite)* of the rear of a Jalpa 350 built to special order by Lamborghini for a customer wanting a personalised car.

CHAPTER 04

Supreme test: the Lamborghini endurance racing car, sponsored by Supreme, which finished fifth on its only outing, in South Africa in 1986.

placed a creditable fifth, was the first with a non-turbo engine to finish.

During the winter following the debut at Kylami, Lamborghini and other manufacturers were focussed on the 1987 season. The championship rules were changed to exclude turbocharged cars because of their dominance and Lamborghini was the only team with an engine that had four valves per cylinder, giving it a theoretical advantage that had to be tested in competition.

At a series of meetings Lamborghini, its UK importer Portman and the sponsors set out a programme to bring the chance of competition success, and the prospect of reward for sponsors' investment. In the end, it never happened and the project was finally scrapped in late 1986 (some said the wisdom of Ferruccio eventually prevailed).

The decision about motor racing was sidelined because Patrick Mimran was deeply involved in a far bigger issue. He was in serious negotiations with the Chrysler Corporation which was interested in buying the company.

At the time, it was common knowledge within Lamborghini and other auto industry circles that Novaro was driven by the ambition of emulating Ferrari and competing in Grand Prix racing. Patrick Mimran was reluctant to commit to the 1987 season, because if his negotiations were successful, Chrysler might not want to be bound by a commitment to a full season of endurance sports car racing in its first year. (Jaguar won the 1987 world championship with an engine using two valves per cylinder that might not have been a match for a Lamborghini).

Patrick Mimran entered the talks with Chrysler following a full review in 1986 of Lamborghini's models and future prospects. Once again, it was essential to match the investment in engines, other components and production with prospects for sales volumes and likely profitability.

This analysis revealed that the Jalpa was not reaching its sales targets and was unlikely ever to do so, even with the benefit of possible upgrades and new derivatives. The Countach Quattrovalvole, Lamborghini's flagship model, continued to be a success and the factory started 1986 with a full order book.

That said, it was apparent to all with experience in the supercar market that there were the first signs that this great car was nearing the end of its production life. Its major problem lay in the aerodynamics and just adding more power was not a solution, because a blunt but realistic assessment would describe the Countach's passage through the air as similar to that of a brick. Lamborghini's next goal was a 200mph model and that would never be possible with the existing Countach.

The LM002 continued to occupy the minds of many at Lamborghini, where confidence survived that a military breakthrough was achievable. Alfieri still had responsibility for this project but the first priority of the engineering department was to work on a replacement Jalpa.

Marmaroli was asked to start designing and building a transverse V12 4-litre engine and this was bench-tested in late 1986. At the same time a prototype Countach was built with a view to improving aerodynamics and reducing weight by using composites in the bodyshell.

This was known as the Evoluzione, an exercise in making the car lighter and more slippery through the air. It was completed in early 1987 and, unpainted, looked stark and to most observers a retrograde step to the Quattrovalvole. The Evoluzione Countach was, though, capable of 190mph, and the prospect of the magical 200mph beckoned, but only one was built and it was never seriously considered for production.

At the time, Lamborghini was collaborating with Gandini who had left the company to work from his own studio with designs carrying his own name. Gandini was commissioned to style and build two vital prototypes: replacements for the Jalpa and the Countach. The replacement Jalpa (codenamed P140 Bravo) was a completely new project with no components to be carried over from the existing Jalpa. The Evoluzione Countach was essentially an in-house development but, as a third project, Gandini also carried out the initial styling of the prototype codenamed LP112 – the car that would in time be named Diablo.

Patrick Mimran could see the development cost of the all-new P140 was going to be high because of the need for new tooling and production facilities. In fact, getting the Jalpa replacement into production was likely to exceed those relating to the Diablo. The Mimrans were committed to giving priority to the P140 because its sales were flagging and unlikely to achieve targets set, whereas strong demand continued for the Countach.

Wealthy as the Mimrans were, they decided the time had come for Lamborghini to relinquish its independence, and become allied to a large manufacturer with far greater resources. Ferrari, always seen as its great rival, was already part of Fiat Auto.

Novaro was charged with contacting a number of manufacturers with a view to gaining a minority shareholding interest from one of them. Chrysler responded positively to Lamborghini's overtures after examining his business plan.

Cash-rich Chrysler was America's third largest vehicle manufacturer behind General Motors and Ford Motor Company, and looked an ideal partner. But the Chrysler executives who evaluated the proposal disagreed with the Mimran business plan.

Chrysler's view was that a supercar manufacturer like Lamborghini should always make its flagship model the top priority when investment in replacements was being debated because it was the most important image maker for the whole range. In other words, said Chrysler, Countach (still selling well) should be replaced before Jalpa (sales in decline).

This fundamental difference of philosophy made Chrysler unwilling to become a minority shareholder and the company decided, in early 1987, to try to negotiate an outright purchase of Nuova Automobili Ferruccio Lamborghini. By May the deal was completed and the Mimrans sold the company (bought for $3m/£1.25m) to the Chrysler Corporation for $33m/£22m after only six years. They saved Lamborghini from extinction and made a handsome profit on their total investment (purchase price plus money injected into the business).

The Mimrans are the only owners to make money out of Lamborghini during its 40-year history, though Audi will hope in time to be the second to find similar success.

"Chrysler began its tenure at Sant'Agata with the financial backing and the will to take Lamborghini on to further success"

As Chrysler took command, nearly everyone ended up happy. The American group was excited by the potential presented by Lamborghini and set about developing a successor to the Countach. They regarded the Evoluzione Countach as surplus to requirements and it ended up in Patrick Mimran's private collection.

Nuova Automobili Ferruccio Lamborghini was now owned by the Chrysler Corporation which transferred its assets to a new trading company, Automobili Lamborghini Spa. The arrival of Chrysler in the boardroom was welcomed by the workforce and Emile Novaro, who had worked the majority of his adult life for the Mimran family and ran Lamborghini for them, was invited by Chrysler to become president of Automobili Lamborghini Spa.

This was a shrewd move by the American group, because he was well liked within Lamborghini and had proved his capability in managing the business. A Frenchman living in Monaco, Novaro was also urbane and experienced, moving easily in the upper echelons of the business and financial sectors.

Chrysler began its tenure at Sant'Agata with the financial backing and the will to take Lamborghini on to further success. The cultural gap that inevitably existed between a big US corporation and an exclusive Italian supercar maker was though to prove divisive.

"The company at last had a parent that could make all the dreams of the factory come true"

05_Dollars do the talking

Chrysler Corporation's $25.2m/£15.36m acquisition of the Fighting Bull in the spring of 1987 must have been greeted with euphoria by virtually every pragmatic Lamborghini lover around the world. The company at last had a parent that could make all the dreams of the factory come true. Little did anyone realise that this was again to be a false dawn, and that seven years later the factory would be left in disarray, devoid of potential new models, buildings half completed, the workforce decimated and the survivors utterly demoralised.

At the outset, the prospects were as warm and sunny as the May weather that blesses northern Italy. Chrysler's president, the legendary Lee Iacocca, was the son of Italian immigrants and moved from Ford after many years when he tangled with Henry Ford II.

He moved to head Chrysler when it was close to bankruptcy and negotiated a huge loan from the US government to perform a miraculous turnaround. He somehow managed to repay the government loan ahead of schedule.

Great day: the Anniversary Countach creates excitement at an owners' club weekend to celebrate the first 25 years of Lamborghini as a supercar manufacturer.

CHAPTER 05

When Chrysler took over at Lamborghini, Iacocca's track record and autocratic style meant that few executives on the main board in Detroit were challenging his decisions. It is hardly surprising that the decision to acquire the Italian exotic sports car maker was officially 'unanimous'. Iacocca certainly received wholehearted support from Bob Lutz, a main board member with deep knowledge of the automobile industry in both the USA and Europe.

Iacocca was known to be a great admirer of all things from the country of his ancestors. Word soon circulated within Chrysler that Iacocca started a crash course in Italian as soon as the ink was dry on the contract. He was already a wine collector and bought a vineyard in Tuscany to strengthen his links with Italy.

Iacocca's enthusiasm for this small but thrilling division of his empire was apparent from the start, in part because it expanded Chrysler's interests in the Mediterranean region.

Chrysler also had a shareholding in Maserati and De Tomaso but at the press conference called to announce its acquisition, Iacocca announced with pride that 'Automobili Lamborghini is the jewel in Chrysler's crown'.

Events were to move swiftly once Chrysler had acquired the assets of Lamborghini. Step one was to set up a structure ensuring Lamborghini could be managed effectively, while the board in Detroit kept a firm hold on strategy and direction.

Chrysler directors were appointed to the board of Lamborghini, and its president, Emile Novaro, and Tony Richards, president of the corporation's European operations, worked in tandem. Franco Ferraris, Lamborghini's finance director, was apparently in charge of spending but in reality could do little without the agreement of Bob Smith, the Chrysler director responsible for business development.

The day-to-day Lamborghini management was in strong hands, with all the key people anxious to work with Chrysler. They included Giulio Alfieri, Luigi Marmiroli, Gianfranco Venturelli and Massimo Ceccarani (all with technical or production responsibilities), and Ubaldo Sgarzi, who continued to head the sales department.

Chrysler closely surveyed its acquisition and the potential global market for exclusive sports cars like Lamborghinis (extra premium, in industry language), which it estimated at about 5,000 a year. A third of those were in the USA, which was one of the attractions of the deal from Chrysler's viewpoint. Lamborghini's rivals were identified as Ferrari, Porsche, Lotus and Aston Martin.

Internal Chrysler memos show that three strategies were considered for Lamborghini. One was 'independent, self-funded growth': the company would develop through the use of

Pressing ahead: Sandro Munari (above), twice winner of the world rally championship driving a Lancia Stratos, joined Lamborghini as its press officer.

Flying start: Mauro Forghieri (left) was recruited from Ferrari when Lamborghini began developing Formula One engines

its own financial resources. Chrysler's judged this 'the least risk path, offering no potential for an adequate return on our $25m (£18m) investment'.

Immediate exploitation of the brand was also short-listed – developing a car 'that was not a genuine Lamborghini', capable of selling 10,000 a year. A briefing document added: 'It is important under this alternative to consider the risk of brand name erosion through exploitation of the name on lower-priced cars through volume dealerships.'

Chrysler chose the third way, called 'independent accelerated growth'. The group would aggressively fund expansion, with the objective of Lamborghini achieving parity with Ferrari (in size, product range and image) in the shortest possible time.

Adequate investment would be coupled with technical and design support, and 1991 was set as the target date for a new car to challenge the Ferrari 328.

Lee Iacocca and his senior colleagues also wanted the glamour of Lamborghini to put a shine on the Chrysler product range in the USA. They wanted to develop a Lamborghini

CHAPTER 05

Beached buggy: inside the LM002, which Lamborghini saw a coastal plaything for the wealthy, and as a military vehicle.

Under control: Chrysler insisted on deposits with orders for the Diablo (right)

engine that would be used in a Chrysler/AMC product equivalent to Italy's Lancia Thema 8.32, which was powered by a Ferrari V8 engine.

Significantly, as things turned out, Chrysler saw the potential dangers at the time. A confidential memo summarised the chosen strategy like this: 'This alternative is a fairly high-risk plan, in that it attempts to equal in five or six years something that took Ferrari more than 25 years of deliberate growth.

'It is, however, the alternative that maximises the value of Lamborghini as an asset for future use ... of the name which will by then have the inherent strength to provide long-term benefit to the corporation.'

Chrysler intended to achieve a production volume of 2,500 cars a year by the end of 1992. Later, as optimism grew, the target was raised to 3,000 but then the market slumped in the global recession at the start of the 1990s, and the figure was trimmed to 1,500.

The plan to increase the number of cars produced at Sant'Agata provided new ammunition for the pro-racing faction, which argued that the factory would need nothing less than the prestige of Formula One. The business plan, put to Chrysler in 1987 and accepted by Iacocca and his board, proposed building engines for Grand Prix teams. To achieve this, Chrysler decided to create a new company, Lamborghini Engineering Spa, managed by Danielle Audetto with Emile Novaro as president. Lamborghini Engineering was given a start-up budget of $5/£2.9m and rented offices in Modena.

Many people at Sant'Agata told Richards and Novaro they doubted whether it would be possible to market a Formula One engine successfully as a joint Chrysler/Lamborghini venture. Richards was given the important role of liaising between Lamborghini and Chrysler as the project took shape, and he and Novaro managed to convince Iacocca that both companies would benefit worldwide from this collaboration.

They also persuaded Iacocca that designing and producing the Grand Prix engine would be financed by the competing teams – it was to be a self-funding venture, just like the offshore powerboat engine. Iacocca believed them.

Audetto's first recruit, Mauro Forghieri, came from arch rival Ferrari and it was something of a coup: his reputation in motorsport was at the genius level. While team manager of Ferrari's Formula One team, Audetto had employed Forghieri as a designer when Nikki Lauda was the star driver.

The timing of the move to Lamborghini was perfect for Forghieri, as he was no longer involved in the Ferrari race programme. Instead, he had been moved to working on special

CHAPTER 05

projects like the Ferrari F40, and the opportunity to return to racing was irresistible, especially as it came with the backing of Chrysler. After 20 years, he severed his connection with Ferrari and, to the added annoyance of his previous employer took two colleagues to Lamborghini in mid 1987.

Forghiere immediately began to design a 3.5 V12, engine, the format he believed was the most appropriate for the Formula. Chrysler did not want the F1 engine project to be undertaken within Sant'Agata (perhaps Ferruccio's views about it being a distraction were remembered) and all the machining and construction work was subcontracted to specialist firms.

In April 1987, the Sant'Agata team set about their tasks with enthusiasm but were behind time, because the negotiations with Chrysler had delayed work on the Diablo, replacement for the Countach.

Key members of the press, dealers and factory personnel were invited to express their opinion about a name. The majority wanted the car to be named after Diablo, a particularly ferocious bull that died in the Madrid bullring in the 19th century and was an important part of Spain's bull-fighting heritage.

At the same time, there was an urgent need to replace the Jalpa (the Mimrans had authorised the project), and in 1986 Marmiroli's department developed the V10, 4-litre

Making a splash: Lamborghini aimed for motorsport success to match the achievements of its engines in the world powerboat championship.

> "Chrysler's failure to deliver the promise it offered to Lamborghini, its workforce, owners and other enthusiasts was lamentable"

engine for the new model. Even so, progress had been slow on the new car, which was referred to as P140 within Lamborghini but was always known to dealers as the Bravo, a name owned by the company and one they liked.

Under the Chrysler business plan, the factory was told to concentrate on getting Diablo into production with all possible haste. Chrysler drew up plans to increase the production area by around 20 per cent and acquired more farmland around the existing factory.

The intention was to complete this work by the end of 1989 to embrace new production lines, plant and equipment, new paint shop and a quality control department. Existing research and development and customer services were revamped and the programme included an expansion of Pagani's composite department for the manufacture of body parts.

The original budget for this development was put at $10m/£6.25m. The motivation was Chrysler's business plan to grow the factory to an annual production of 2,500 cars.

Chrysler's failure to deliver the promise it offered to Lamborghini, its workforce, owners and other enthusiasts was lamentable. The proposed development of the production department (mainly the installation of a new line to build P140) was not completed and, seven years later when Lamborghini was sold, the structure remained an empty shell.

Looking back, it is astonishing that a major car manufacturer could fail to ensure the completion of such a relatively modest programme.

Chrysler wanted Lamborghini to start building the Diablo from September 1988, a little under 18 months after the group took control. Four prototypes were built by Gandini over the next two years, embracing body-styling changes in part dictated by Detroit and based on natural evolution during development by Marmiroli's research department.

Even in those early days, there were tensions in the marriage between Chrysler and Lamborghini at a technical level because Sant'Agata's engineers resented Detroit's attempts to influence the styling. The essence of Lamborghini was held dear by all at the factory, and there was no confidence in decisions made by Chrysler which could always have the last word.

More trouble hit Lamborghini during 1987. Emile Novaro, its president, was seriously injured when he lost control of his Mercedes in France when returning at high speed from the Paris motor show. He was trying to avoid a dog that ran across his path and the car rolled several times. Novaro, fortunate to escape with his life, suffered several fractures and other injuries, and it was to take him six months to return to being a full-time member

CHAPTER 05

of the management team. This was a bad blow for all at Lamborghini because he was the one man capable of standing up to Chrysler's head of engineering in Detroit.

The senior executives in Detroit paid the bills, owned the company and felt they had the right to control all aspects of design and production at Lamborghini. They failed to spot the cultural divide that was opening.

By the end of 1987 it was clear that the Diablo could not possibly be ready for production by September 1988 when Lamborghini was to celebrate its 25th anniversary. Instead, an 'ultimate' Countach was to take its place, and work was rapidly undertaken to restyle the car.

Tensions were further deepened at this time when a new competitor entered the market – the Cizeta Moroder, powered by an all-new V16 four-valve engine. Giorgio Moroder, who headed the company, was a wealthy Italian who recruited two talented ex-Lamborghini engineers – Claudio Zampoli and Paulo Stanzani. Marcello Gandini, once a Lamborghini employee but now with his own design studio, styled the Cizeta and the body styling was remarkably similar to the Diablo.

This made Chrysler in Detroit even more determined to enforce major restyling for

Sunny prospect: Monte Carlo was chosen as a suitable setting for the launch of Diablo which proved to be the best-selling Lamborghini before Audi ownership.

Diablo and confidence in Gandini was at a low ebb. Gandini had been given the impression by the Mimrans that Diablo was not going into production and so his design for Cizeta was a natural evolution from his studio.

Things then changed fast: the newcomer went out of business after building only about seven cars. Chrysler agreed to commit to Gandini for the Diablo as the model was at advanced stage of development.

Work continued on the Anniversary Countach and, at a slower pace, on the Diablo. In the absence of the injured Novaro, Chrysler sent its executive Carl Levy from Detroit to run Lamborghini, reporting to Bob Smith and Tony Richards.

Levy was told to try to keep the Chrysler business plan on track but neither Smith nor Richards was strong enough to allow the factory the freedom to develop the Diablo as they wished.

The 25th anniversary of Lamborghini presented Chrysler with a great marketing opportunity, and the board in Detroit seized it with enthusiasm. Danielle Audetto was asked to organise a spectacular owners' club weekend at Salsomaggiore, a health spa near Palma, in September 1988.

At times, disagreements had flared into full-blooded arguments, but the Chrysler main board was still very much behind Lamborghini. The anniversary party was seen as the ideal opportunity for the Chrysler president, Lee Iacocca, to meet the world's press, dealers and representatives of owners' clubs. He could spell out the details of the business plan and outline Chrysler's ambitions for Lamborghini.

The event was memorable for the 600 people who attended and about 140 Lamborghinis were there as well. The focal point was a formal gala dinner hosted by Lee Iacocca who was willing to be upstaged by the guest of honour he introduced. To the delight of all, Ferruccio Lamborghini walked to the microphone to wish Chrysler well with its acquisition.

Chrysler used the occasion to have private talks with Ferruccio and invite him to return to Lamborghini in an honorary position. There would have been an obvious marketing benefit but the founder gracefully declined the invitation. Ferruccio later told former colleagues: "I do not want to be brought out and dusted off as a promotional person – my era is history."

Ferruccio would have been the first to say that the real star of the weekend was the Anniversary Countach, the work of Marmiroli and Pagani who cleverly restyled the

CHAPTER 05

bodyshell and the interior. A major redesign of the suspension was also needed to accommodate new low-profile Pirelli P Zero tyres.

The P Zero underscored Lamborghini's close relationship with Pirelli and the Anniversary Countach was the first production car to use the tyre as original equipment. Former rally driver Sandro Munari, best known for twice winning the world championship with the Lancia Stratos, had joined Lamborghini as press officer. His talents were used for much of the test driving of the latest Countach.

Production of the Anniversary began in September 1988 and continued until July 1990, with some Lamborghini admirers describing it as the most stylish and driveable derivative of the Countach.

The dealer network instantly underwrote the quoted factory production total of 700 Anniversary cars and so it became a limited edition Countach. Soon after entering showrooms, it was being sold second hand at more than the list price.

Chrysler's ownership was restoring confidence in Lamborghini ownership and the global economic climate was buoyant. Lamborghini could have sold three times as many Countach Anniversary cars as were built, as enthusiasts swiftly bought or ordered all the cars allocated to dealers.

The 25th Lamborghini anniversary also marked the welcome return of Emile Novaro to the factory after a long recovery following his car crash. The 1980s strongman of Lamborghini held a one-to-one meeting with Iacocca, and told the Chrysler president he must use his authority to halt the continued interference in the development of the Diablo, and to give the go-ahead for the P140/Bravo, the Jalpa replacement.

Iacocca was formidable in any business discussion and had become a workaholic since the death of his wife in 1983 after a long illness. He was a larger than life character, who would smoke cigars in any office he visited. He relaxed by playing poker on Friday nights with a group of friends.

Novaro convinced Iacocca that Sant'Agata had to be given its head in developing the Diablo and Bob Gale, head of Chrysler Special Projects, allowed Lamborghini engineers to proceed without interference from Detroit. For all who knew the inside story, this was one of the sweetest moments in Lamborghini's history: the Fighting Bull had shown bravery at a testing time, and won.

Novaro's success was even more impressive because Chrysler was to exhibit a four-door car – 'Chrysler powered by Lamborghini' – at the 1987 Frankfurt motor show. The

"The dealer network instantly underwrote the quoted factory production total of 700 Anniversary cars and so it became a limited edition Countach"

vehicle, named Portofino, was styled by Chrysler's Specifico studio and built by Coggiota of Turin. It embraced Jalpa moving parts and Countach Spider pillar-less doors front and rear. The styling failed to gel with the motoring press and the most favourable description was 'mid Atlantic'.

The Portofino – a market research vehicle – was not received favourably by Lamborghini lovers as something pointing to the future of the marque. Within the factory, employees christened it 'the big potato'. The vehicle's poor reception registered with Chrysler and the project was quickly liquidated. Few mourned its passing, but it meant that Lamborghini's design progression was uncertain.

The Jalpa dropped out of the Lamborghini range in 1988 and in its place (at last) came the Bravo and the car turned out to be much more advanced than previously disclosed. At the time of the Countach 25th Anniversary meeting, three prototypes of P140 were at Sant'Agata for appraisal by Lamborghini and Chrysler.

An inner circle of people were asked to say which prototype they thought should be signed-off for development into a production model. Luigi Marmaroli, the head of engineering, wanted to know which car British buyers would like to see as a replacement for the Jalpa. He was also taking soundings on the likely reception in the USA.

One car stood out. It was from the pen of Gandini, the former Lamborghini designer, who had temporarily lost favour after styling for the short-lived Moroder Cizeta. Lamborghini had, for its 25 years, been searching for a small model, and Gandini's was totally in tune with the heart of the company's philosophy.

A distant number two was a car by Bertone which was not radical enough to carry the Fighting Bull logo. The third prototype, from Detroit, was devoid of any European panache.

The 'baby Lambo' was allocated a $25m/£14.5m research and development budget by Lamborghini with Chrysler's agreement, amid confidence that making and selling more than 2,000 cars a year was realistic. There was space in the range for another car. A prototype named Genesis had been commissioned from Bertone by Lamborghini/Chrysler in 1987, when Gandini was out of favour.

Chrysler's fortunes in America had revived on the success of its MPV range and Bertone's brief was to design a top-of-the-range MPV (multi purpose vehicle), using the Quattrovalvole engine.

The car was on the stand at the Turin motor show in April, 1988, to test public reaction. It was an ingenuous design, with more space and performance than any other MPV, but

Pollution problem: Diablo was approved in all Lamborghini markets apart from the USA, where it failed emission tests.

when the project was reviewed later in the year, it was abandoned because Genesis did not fit into Chrysler's or Lamborghini's production range.

LM002 sales in 1988 continued to be slow and Alfieri was made responsible for developing the model. He was also given the job of increasing sales. Odd variants were evolved to try to exploit different markets in the USA, and these included a 7-litre engine option although most LM002s were sold with the 5.2 QV engine.

In 1989, two special vehicles were built for a Japanese client to take part in the Paris/Dakar rally with a view to proving the LM's off-road capability. It failed to perform well enough to make an impact and there was continuing disappointment in the search for military buyers.

In his bid to land a substantial order, Alfieri spent much of his time in Libya and other Middle East countries but drew a blank. He had been moved sideways from the main research and development department (which was effectively run by Marmaroli) and, probably through no fault of his, Alfieri failed to make LM002 a commercial success.

He was perceived as the man responsible for its creation during the Mimran era, and there was no way back into the engineering department for him. Alfieri was offered a package to take early retirement when aged about 60 and had little option but to accept it.

During 1988, specialist premises were found in Modena that were large enough to accommodate the growth that Audetto and Forghieri anticipated for Lamborghini Engineering and its Formula One engine. Lamborghini Engineering also planned to repeat the policy of the company's powerboat engine division, supplying engines to competing F1 teams on a race-by-race basis. The engines would be rebuilt and upgraded after each race throughout the season.

Enthusiastic support from Chrysler European boss Tony Richards ensured that Lamborghini was well funded at this time, and Lamborghini Engineering was able to invest in people, plant and equipment at its Modena base. A further encouraging sign was Chrysler's agreement to supply the vital hi-tech computer support and personnel that was becoming so vital in Formula One.

The engine was ready for dynamometer testing (to assess its power) by the end of 1988. Development continued at a remarkably rapid rate and the engine – developing more 600bhp – was ready for racing in the spring of 1989. It made its debut in a Lola-bodied Larousse team car in the March at the Argentine Grand Prix with drivers Philippe Aliot and Yanack Delmas.

Lotus was not quite the force it had been in previous years but with determined and competitive drivers Derek Warwick and Martin Donnelly in the cars, and major backing from Camel, much was expected of the team. Both teams earned championship points in 1990, though they struggled to meet their contractual obligations to Lamborghini.

During the season, Lamborghini Engineering approached Portman, the UK distributor, with a view to organising a team to compete in the world endurance sports car series. Portman commissioned a prototype from Spice Engineering at Silverstone, the UK race circuit, and, with sponsorship from ASK, a Japanese design group, prepared a small, light and extremely quick endurance racing car.

The car was tested with Lamborghini engines at two circuits – Donington Park in the UK, and France's Paul Ricard – and at each beat class lap records held by Mercedes-Benz.

Too often, in the 40 years of Lamborghini, progress has been swiftly followed by bitter disappointment. This happened again, when Spice Engineering went into receivership, forcing Lamborghini to scrap its commitment to Formula One and endurance racing.

During Chrysler's stewardship, progress in the Lamborghini marine engine division (set up under the Mimrans) continued steadily. This was mainly under the management of Giuseppe Girotti, supported by a highly competent small engineering division.

An update of the four-overhead-valve version of the L804 marine engine, revealed in 1988, proved to be a winner. Lamborghini developed the L804 to take advantage of a change in the rules by UIM, organiser of powerboat racing, to increase the size to 8172cc but they were also able to boost the power to 880bhp at 6650rpm. The engineers concentrated on the power to weight ratio – the classic V12, 60-degree configuration was retained, but built entirely of lightweight aluminium.

The engine was used extensively for the next three years with great success in the world and European championships. Production of the L804 reached 75 a year and all were supplied to teams under an agreement that after each race, the engine was returned to the factory for a rebuild.

The division also developed a petrol-driven marine engine marketed as the 'ultimate' in powering leisure craft. This L900 engine was a derivative of the 12-cylinder competition version and the specification was changed to make it more suited to a high performance leisure craft. The result was a 9300cc engine, with an output of 630bhp at 5300rpm.

The performance of the L900 aroused interest from many marine manufacturers, including the market leader, Mercury Performance Products, based in Wisconsin, USA.

In 1989, after extensive tests, Danielle Audetto negotiated for Lamborghini a contract to sell to Mercury up to 1,000 units, with the camshaft cover bearing the names of both Mercury and Lamborghini. On the strength of this agreement, Lamborghini built an additional production line at Sant'Agata. To the disappointment of both companies, the recession savaged demand for high-value pleasure craft experienced in the USA from 1990 onwards and Mercury failed to take up its commitment. The contract was cancelled in 1992.

Even so, the marine competition department was outstandingly successful, with every prestige race won at least once by boats powered by Lamborghini engines.

Lamborghini-powered boats have won both the world and European power boat championships a number of times, and the company remains actively involved in the sport. Over the course of some 20 years of racing, Lamborghini has become to offshore power boat racing what Ferrari is to Formula 1. There's a double irony in that, given Ferruccio's

Diablo day: the launch of the model was referred to as 'Lamborghini Day 2' by Chrysler which wanted to emphasise that this was a new dawn for Sant'Agata.

determination to produce better road cars than Ferrari, while maintaining to his death passionate opposition to Lamborghini competing in motor sport.

The skilful management of the marine division in 1990 was in marked contrast to events elsewhere in Lamborghini. In one of the most extraordinary episodes in the company's chequered history, a mysterious Mexican industrialist had meetings with the company and (apparently) agreed to underwrite, for six months, the $25m/£13.8m needed for the team to compete in Formula One. Chrysler then agreed to underwrite the budget until the Mexican's money arrived.

CHAPTER 05

Forghieri and his team pressed ahead to design a chassis, engine and transmission in time for the car to participate in the 1991 F1 season. Amazingly Lamborghini was unable to trace the Mexican benefactor who seemed to vanish. Chrysler executives were not amused.

The entire project had been ill-conceived and left the Lamborghini executives embarrassed by their naivety, but Audetto and Lamborghini found a saviour.

Carlo Patrucco, president of the Fini, a major Italian food and hotel group, and colleagues from the Confederation of Italian Industry stepped in and agreed to part-fund the operation and support Team Modena Lamborghini, which at its birth employed more than 100 people.

In the early 1990s, Formula One had more entrants than places on the starting grid and the lesser teams competed in pre-qualification at the start of practice. Larini and Van Der Poole, the Lamborghini drivers, struggled to qualify and Chrysler's interest in supporting these expensive racing exploits was waning. Then funds were cut off, which meant the team was unable to complete the season.

At the end of the 1991 F1 season, following a review by Chrysler, Mauro Forghieri was asked to leave, with Lamborghini Engineering working only on a Formula One engine. This seemed to be further proof of Ferruccio's good judgement that Lamborghini should never have been tempted to enter Formula One racing.

During 1989 and 1990, Lamborghini existed on the expectation of better times ahead. The LM002 continued to find a few private buyers but the factory was once again reliant on one model, the Anniversary Countach. A full order book for this car, the need to upgrade the older Lamborghinis and the development of Bravo and Diablo meant the plant was working flat-out. There were grounds for optimism.

On December 5, 1989, the new research and development facility was officially finished and the number of engineers on Lamborghini's payroll rose to 80. Chrysler could begin to see the prospect of a payback on its investment and, following Iacocca's intervention, its engineers appeared to respect Novaro's request for autonomy during the development of Lamborghini models.

Iacocca's decision was not solely to assist with the advancement of Lamborghini, because he knew it was important for his engineering team in Detroit to concentrate on the Chrysler product, as its market share was weakening in the USA.

At Sant'Agata, the priority remained the development of the definitive Diablo, powered by a V12 engine, with the cubic capacity increased to 5707cc and developing 520bhp at

> "In the short-term, this was a time for celebration - a rapturous reception for Diablo, Iacocca's insistence on Lamborghini autonomy and money in the bank"

7100rpm, with a top speed of around 190mph/325kph, with Lamborghini fuel injection.

The coming launch of Diablo brought about a break in Lamborghini tradition: it was decided not to unveil it at Geneva, Europe's spring motor show, which attracts global attention. Instead, decided Chrysler, it would be better to stage something individual, drawing on the success of the 25th anniversary party at Salsomaggiore.

The launch of Diablo was referred to as 'Lamborghini Day 2' to suggest a new dawn for the company under Chrysler. January 20, 1990, was chosen for the occasion and there was mounting pressure on the team at Sant'Agata to have the car ready.

This was the most flamboyant launch staged by Lamborghini, with around 500 guests attending a gala dinner at the Monte Carlo Sporting Club. They were the first to glimpse the Diablo, which emerged through a cloud of dry ice after the emotional rendition of a number of songs by José Carreras, one of Italy's 'three tenors'. Many other Lamborghini enthusiasts were able to see the Diablo on display the following day.

The dinner was attended by VIPs from around the world including Malcolm Forbes of Forbes Publishing and former racing driver Mario Andretti, a son of Italy. Lee Iacocca, joint host with Emile Novaro, used the event to emphasise Chrysler's commitment to the growth and success of Lamborghini.

First deliveries of the Diablo were set for September 1990 and Iacocca took advantage of the strong order book by saying anyone wanting a car to be built in 1990 or 1991 would need to pay a $42,500/£25,000 deposit. Within a few months of the Monte Carlo launch, orders were secured for the first 600 Diablos, and Lamborghini banked deposits totalling around $25m/£15m which represented a remarkable fillip to the company's cashflow.

In the short-term, this was a time for celebration - a rapturous reception for Diablo, Iacocca's insistence on Lamborghini autonomy and money in the bank.

But life is rarely this simple in the automotive industry and the birth of the 1990s brought the first breezes of an icy wind of change that was to blow through global economies. Few could have fully realised the challenges ahead that were to buffet Lamborghini: the Fighting Bull was about to be in danger of being blown off its feet as Chrysler Corporation, its parent, prepared to face a grim fight for its own survival as an independent group.

"Little Lamborghini in northern Italy slipped even further down the list when it came to allocating investment"

06_Coup de grace for Bravo; farewell Chrysler

Manufacturers of popular cars are among the first to be damaged by an economic slump - delay in buying the next new auto is a popular first move when you need to tighten personal or business finances. The global recession that loomed into view in 1990 was to bite at a time when Chrysler Corporation was vulnerable, and little Lamborghini in northern Italy slipped even further down the list when it came to allocating investment.

Lamborghini, Ferrari and other car makers for the rich viewed the recession with concern but did not feel the effects of the initial downturn. Demand for Lamborghini's new and used cars continued at a healthy rate until the end of 1991.

Production of Diablo started in September, 1990, and the car had cleared type approval tests everywhere apart from the USA, where it failed to meet the new lower level of harmful exhaust emission gases. Crash simulations were completed at Britain's MIRA test centre without throwing up any fresh problems.

End of the line: production of the Anniversary Countach stopped in July 1990 so that the first Diablos would be built in the September of that year.

CHAPTER 06

America was expected to take 40 per cent of Lamborghini production and Chrysler built a new import centre in Florida. This was an important investment and costs were ramped up by the decision to ensure that the site reflected Lamborghini's image. Large smoked glass windows and interior fittings blended to match Lamborghini's exclusive image.

Chrysler decided the import centre would carry out the final certification of type approval for cars on their way to US buyers. The policy was vehemently opposed by Ubaldo Sgarzi, Lamborghini's sales supremo, who suspected that Chrysler was handing franchises to sell Diablo and other cars in the range to the most successful Chrysler outlets in the States. Some of these dealerships were huge, and Sgazi protested that a solitary Lamborghini would be lost in premises where 1,000 vehicles were for sale. Chrysler was in danger of grossly devaluing Lamborghini in its most important market.

Sgarzi, who had overseen distribution since the birth of Lamborghini, was passionate about the need to appoint dealers with the interest, knowledge and resources to give owners the aftersales service they demanded. Ferruccio had understood that, and encouraged European owners to take their cars back to Sant'Agata for service work. Sgarzi knew that for Lamborghini customers in America, Chrysler's policy was a disaster, as knowledge of the product and the ability to service the cars were proving virtually non-existent.

Chrysler was looking for the best way of recouping the money it was putting into Lamborghini and setting out to make its subsidiary profitable as quickly as possible.

Completing the development of the Diablo in 1989 and 1990 cost Chrysler around $5.1m/£3m by the time the first car was delivered to a customer. This included completing the VT four-wheel-drive Diablo, which started production in mid -1991. The VT used the same components as the initial Diablo, apart from drive-line changes.

On December 6, 1989, a new research and development facility was opened in the south-eastern area of the plant, employing 80 engineers. The last Anniversary Countach went down the assembly line in July 1990 and the first production Diablos were completed at the end of September.

Just when Lamborghini prepared to capitalise on its latest model, a raft of teething problems prevented the factory releasing the first 80 Diablos to enthusiasts who had paid their deposits of $42,500/£25,000 and were eager to drive their car. Most of these early cars were due to be shipped to the USA.

The factory did its best to hush this up. The Diablo's engine was overheating, and there were problems with the brakes: the quality was well below the level expected in an

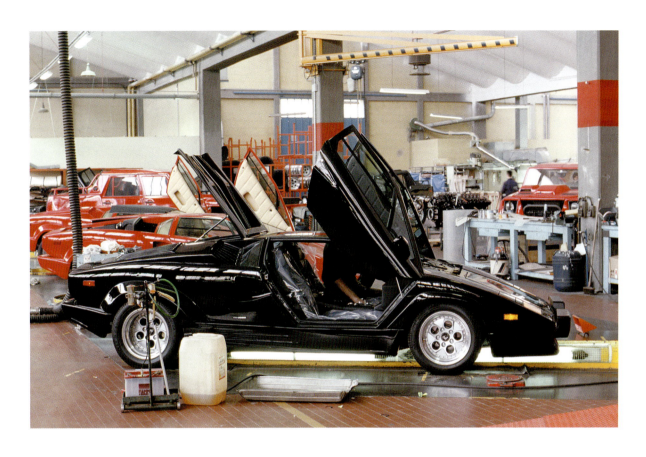

USA bound: Anniversary Countach production *(above)* **– the black car in the foreground was to be sold in America, a key overseas market for Lamborghini.**

Distributor problem: Ubaldo Sgarzi *(left)* **reacted badly to the decision to scrap Bravo, taking early retirement.**

ordinary car, let alone such an exclusive one.

Lamborghini was forced to resolve the problems by moving many of the engineers employed in the research and development department to the production line as trouble shooters. The disastrous knock-on effect was to delay the development of the already overdue P140/Bravo by a further six months.

The first right-hand-drive Diablo was not completed until June 1991. By then Portman, the sole UK importer and dealer, should have been receiving a steady flow of cars for delivery to buyers by agreed dates. In 1988, Chrysler's Tony Richards and Emile Novaro had stressed to Portman that a condition of being sole British importer was the need to expand its business to sell the 300 right-hand-drive cars that the factory was then committed to building each year. Richards regarded effective distribution as a Lamborghini 'balance sheet item' and so insisted that it was essential for the factory to put in place a worldwide dealer network capable of selling the production objective of 3,000 cars a year.

105

CHAPTER 06

In the frame: early morning mist forms a backcloth for the dashing lines of Diablo.

106

"By 1991, the recession was biting and Chrysler's credibility problems were starting to tarnish the image of Lamborghini"

Portman, which had committed to supporting Chrysler's business plan for the expansion of Lamborghini, bought land at Brooklands, which in the 1930s had been a motor racing circuit. The site is on the outskirts of London close to the M25, the capital's orbital motorway. In early 1990, building work began there on a Lamborghini sales, parts and service centre.

The relationship between Lamborghini's and Chrysler's engineering departments had cooled at the time of the Diablo launch, but the Chrysler board continued to state commitment to Lamborghini, its dealers and the clients.

But, unknown to Lamborghini, some members of the Chrysler board viewed the effects of the recession biting into the automobile industry, worried about Chrysler's future and saw Lamborghini as an increasingly expensive toy.

In January 1990 JP Morgan, the US merchant bank, was instructed by Chrysler to work confidentially to find someone to purchase Lamborghini. All major motor manufacturers were approached about Project Saint and, inevitably, rumours began to circulate.

By 1991, the recession was biting and Chrysler's credibility problems were starting to tarnish the image of Lamborghini. Doubts arose about whether Lamborghinis would hold their value at a level acceptable to potential buyers. It all felt like déjà vu: the future of Lamborghini seemed again to be sliding into uncertainty.

For Lamborghini, 1991 was a critical year. Chrysler was looking for a purchaser but needed to maintain some investment, otherwise its subsidiary would be impossible to sell. Tony Richards, Chrysler's European boss, went to his main board in Detroit and made out a case for the group to give $25m/£14.5m to sustain the development of P140/Bravo and continue the work of the research and development department.

Interest in Lamborghini was waning in the Chrysler boardroom and from mid 1991 onwards, Richards was fighting for sufficient cash to keep Lamborghini alive.

Chrysler hoped to prove it was keeping its nerve by giving the go ahead for Gandini to design a roadster version of the Diablo, using components from the VT, and the car was ready in time for the 1992 Geneva motor show. The car never went into production because no suitable soft hood was available, and talks about this with Chrysler came to nothing.

In early 1992, the board at last agreed to increase its investment in Lamborghini, but limited this to $5m/£2.7m for P140/Bravo, which was merely a fifth of what Tony Richards regarded as necessary. He had thought he convinced the sceptics on the board that any prospective buyer of Lamborghini would need new products in the pipeline.

CHAPTER 06

No soft option: Diablo was a great success as a coupe *(above)* **but the idea of a roadster was dropped when Lamborghini failed to find a suitable roof.**

Local admirer: a resident of Sant'Agata gazes at a Diablo SE *(above right)* **parked outside her home near the Lamborghini factory.**

Lamborghini was under the impression the payment secured by Richards was the first instalment towards the total cost of getting the P140/Bravo into showrooms, and that more money would follow from Detroit.

Believing it had been given the green light by Detroit, Sant'Agata decided to press ahead with the Gandini version of Bravo. They set a revised delivery date of 1994 and this was to be announced on Lamborghini Day 3 in 1993, when 30 years of Lamborghini would be celebrated.

Portman arranged the crash testing of the Bravo prototype at MIRA and Lamborghini

placed an order for the composite aluminium chassis and bodyshells. When Chrysler learnt of the contract, it immediately cancelled Bravo, prompting Vehma Inc (which had already tooled up for the production) to threaten to sue to recover its costs.

The matter never went to court because Chrysler was able to negotiate its way out of a damaging position, using as a lever the amount of business it conducted in the USA with the parent company. But Chrysler had to write off the $20m/£13m spent on Bravo.

For Chrysler, communicating that the investment had been a total and not an interim sum should have been straightforward. Its failure to do so has never been fully explained and was, at best, a dreadful misunderstanding, which caused serious repercussions.

Ubaldo Sgarzi, aware of dealer enthusiasm for the car, reacted badly to the news that Bravo would be scrapped, although Chrysler insisted it was merely on temporary hold. He decided he no longer wanted to work for Lamborghini after running the sales department for nearly 30 years, and opted for early retirement, so that he could enjoy the benefits of the Chrysler-managed pension fund.

He left at the end of 1992. Sgarzi was then able to start enjoying travel to pursue his own interests (including finding additions to his art collection), rather than fostering Lamborghini's all over the world. He had a particular love of Africa, and was to spend a good deal of time in Kenya.

Sgarzi was replaced by Giuseppe Girotti, who had previously worked at Lamborghini as an engineer procuring parts from suppliers during the Mimran days. On his return to Sant'Agata from Ferrari, he ran the service and parts operation and was also managing the offshore powerboat engine division.

The future for Lamborghini continued to look uncertain in 1992. Its president, Emile Novaro, had somehow failed to recognise that demand for expensive cars like Lamborghinis had by now become badly damaged by the global slowdown. He also seemed oblivious to the damage to Lamborghini's reputation caused by constant rumours in the press that the manufacturer had become a burden to Chrysler, whose aim was to rid themselves of their Italian investments.

Any lingering hopes that Chrysler's main board might change its mind about disposing of Lamborghini disappeared at the end of 1992 when Lee Iacocca departed as chairman of Chrysler: Lamborghini had lost its champion.

The position at Sant'Agata was becoming ever more depressing, with 94 unsold Diablos a daily and painful reminder of the change of fortune. Each also represented a deposit that never arrived to ease cash flow. In September 1992, production ground to a halt and much of the labour force was made redundant or put on part-time. Lamborghini abided by Italian labour laws, paying some people the equivalent of 20 hours a week not to turn up for work.

Chrysler continued its support for the F1 engine programme in 1992 and Forghieri was replaced by Chrysler's Mike Royce from Detroit as head of engineering. During that season, Lamborghini supplied engines to the Minardi and Lieger teams, which struggled to meet their contractual obligations.

The crucial year for Lamborghini Engineering was 1993 when Adams and Audetto

Floral tribute: Diablo's V12 engine which, for the GTR derivative, produced 590bhp at 7300rpm.

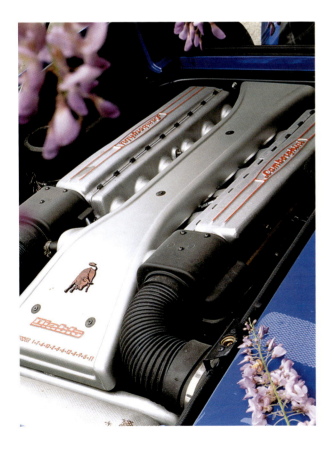

recognised it was necessary to supply one of the major and well funded teams. They agreed a test programme with McLaren, with a view to the two companies joining forces for the 1994 season. Seven engines were prepared in August 1993 using McLaren's TAG injection systems.

In September, testing started with Ayrton Senna and Mika Hakkinen driving cars based on a modified McLaren chassis. Minardi and Benetton both said they were interested in an engine supply deal.

In October 1993, Adams and Audetto visited McLaren team boss Ron Dennis at his home in the south of France to sign a new engine agreement. Dennis insisted that Lamborghini built engines exclusively for McLaren because he did not want its expertise to be shared with his rivals.

Audetto, relying only on McLaren's verbal acceptance of the agreement, told Benetton and other teams expressing an interest that Lamborghini would be unable to supply them during 1993. A few weeks later, Audetto heard from McLaren that Peugeot had agreed to supply it with free engines, and so the arrangement with Lamborghini was off.

Audetto tried to resurrect the deals with Benetton and others, to be told they had concluded deals with Ford Cosworth and other suppliers. This lack of business sense left Lamborghini with no team to use its engine, and presented Tony Richards with the unenviable task of reporting the sorry state of affairs to Chrysler. The board had run out of patience, announcing the end of Lamborghini Engineering and the closure of the plant.

There was other cause for gloom at Sant'Agata in 1993. On February 20, came word of the death of founder Ferruccio Lamborghini, shortly before his 76th birthday, and a few weeks after the onset of heart problems. Many who did business with Ferruccio respected his enterprise and tremendous drive, but his vision for Lamborghini never quite materialised during his lifetime. He died a happy man, for he found growing grapes a satisfying replacement for his earlier life as the creator of a legendary car marque.

His death brought yet another twist in the tale of Lamborghini when Ferruccio's collection of seven Lamborghini cars passed to his son Tonino, together with the two businesses making air conditioning units and hydraulic valves.

There had already been tension between Tonino and Lamborghini/Chrysler when he started to market clothing and accessories under the Lamborghini name. This was centred on the use by Tonino of the Lamborghini logo used from day one on the cars. Chrysler had assumed the logo was included when it purchased Lamborghini, but this was not so.

Tonino opened retail shops in London, Paris and Milan with plans to expand in the US and other countries. Chrysler maintained Tonino's product range was in conflict with its own programme for marketing fashion goods under the Lamborghini brand name. Lawyers must have been rubbing their hands in gleeful expectation of a bitter legal battle, but a sensible solution was reached out of court, with Tonino marketing his product as Tonino Lamborghini and changing the logo.

The sole pleasant distraction in 1993 came in the September. Day 3 celebrated 30 years of Lamborghini, staged primarily at the factory, but with an event at the Modena Aeroclub. The traditional unveiling of a new car on such occasions was no more than a token gesture, for the Diablo SE was a lightweight version with a little more performance. Chrysler's heart was not in this marketing exercise. Marmaroli shed weight from the Diablo (the SE was 250 kilos lighter than the VT) by removing the air conditioning unit, electric windows and other features, which were then offered back as optional extras. The Diablo was also made lighter by replacing its 4x4 transmission with rear-wheel drive. This was the best Lamborghini could manage on an important anniversary.

In 1993, Lamborghini Engineering proved to be another financial drain on Chrysler's stretched financial resources. The company operated separately from the car maker and was created largely through the energy of Emile Novaro, who in March resigned as president of Lamborghini, a month after Ferruccio's death.

Novaro, appointed by the Mimrans, convinced the incoming Chrysler he was the man to continue in the hot seat but the global recession had dramatically changed the Lamborghini agenda. The lack of demand for its cars, unsold stock and the continuing wage bill contributed to a loss of $15m/£25m in 1993. Chrysler wanted to be rid of Sant'Agata,

Into Novaro's position stepped Timothy Adams, an American product marketing executive from Chrysler Europe, whose brief was to dispose of Lamborghini speedily. Adams had been reporting to Tony Richards who moved to head AMC (American Motor Corporation) in America. AMC, responsible for the original Willys Jeep, was later absorbed by Chrysler Jeep, now part of DaimlerChrysler.

Press speculation intensified following the change at the top, and Adams often came under pressure from journalists, business associates and employees to explain what was happening at Lamborghini. His words to fend off questions about the company's future might have been written by a politican: 'All things are possible. Chrysler might still sell if the right offer were to materialise. Or we might keep the factory, as we believe in its future'.

After a while, Adams began to like Lamborghini and his determination to find a buyer who would invest in the company grew stronger by the day. He had discrete talks with several car manufacturers as he tried to meet the board's demand. Some of the potential targets were put off by the sad state of the company, following all the optimism at the beginning of Chrysler's ownership that was never realised.

Then Adams found the man he wanted – Tommy Suharto, son of the then president of Indonesia. Suharto's business interests included engineering companies and the prospect of owning something as glamorous as Lamborghini appealed to him. Soon, it came down to how much he would have to pay.

Bob Eaton, president of Chrysler Corporation, felt it was time to dispose of Automobili Lamborghini Spa, Lamborghini Engineering and Lamborghini USA Inc. There was little opposition among his board colleagues and Eaton rubber stamped the sale of the companies to Megatech Spa.

Chrysler owned Lamborghini for seven years and it is estimated to have cost the group around $60m/£40m. Eaton was to go on and lead the negotiations that ended with the merger of Chrysler and Daimler Benz, creating DaimlerChrysler.

Sales success: Lamborghini built 2,097 Diablos (including this VT derivative) between 1990 and 1998.

"It was a period when the English took over day-to-day control of Lamborghini, which had been true to its Italian roots even during the Chrysler era"

07_ The Brits and Megatech: imperfect harmony

After its sale to an Indonesian syndicate, Lamborghini was to be headed by a man whose behaviour was often eccentric, occasionally bizarre. This was not Tommy Suharto, son of the country's president, but Mike Kimberley, a British automotive industry executive, who riled the workforce at Sant'Agata when he was experienced enough to have known better. It was a period when the English took over day-to-day control of Lamborghini, which had been true to its Italian roots even during the Chrysler era (the boss, remember, learnt to speak the language and purchased a vineyard).

In January 1994, the Indonesian consortium of Megatech, Sedtco and V'Power paid a reported $25m/£16.5m for Automobili Lamborghini Spa and Lamborghini Engineering. Megatech held 80 per cent of the shares, Sedtco and V'Power about 10 per cent each.

Chrysler's two senior Sant'Agata executives, Tim Adams (president of Automobili) and Mike Royce (development manager of Lamborghini Engineering) returned to the USA and took up new posts with the company.

Bridging the years: the 350 GT, introduced in 1964, and the Diablo which made its debut in 1990.

CHAPTER 07

Tommy Suharto, more formally known as Hutomo Mandala Putra, headed a new board of directors as Lamborghini's president, and was also the boss of the consortium, owning a controlling interest in the two other companies.

Suharto was supported by Setjawan Djodi, a close business associate of his father, and a powerful figure in his own right in Indonesia, through his financial dealings and political influence. Gianfranco Ventorelli, the production director in Chrysler days, remained on the board and Franco Ferraris stayed on as finance director. Megatech and its associates acquired Automobili Lamborghini Spa, Lamborghini Engineering and Lamborghini USA.

The viability of Automobili Lamborghini was dependent on production of the Diablo VT and Diablo Special Equipment, with further revenue and profit coming from the group's growing Marine Engine Division. In 1994, Megatech's first year, just over 200 Diablos were built, too few even to justify a labour force that had been reduced to around 400 during the final two years of Chrysler's ownership. Also, Lamborghini could not rely on income from motor racing, following Minardi's decision in 1993 to take its business to Cosworth Ford: there were no immediate prospects of supplying engines to any Grand Prix teams.

Lamborghini's engineering section had done its best to win subcontracted specialist design work, but with little success and the departure of Forghieri and Royce left the company without an engineering leader. Changes to Formula 1 regulations were on the horizon, with the engine size to be reduced from 3.5 litres to 3.0. This meant that if Lamborghini was to stay on the pace in F1 engine production, investment was needed to develop a new 3-litre engine. Nor did prospects look any brighter for Lamborghini's road cars – Megatech had not acquired a single commercially-viable design in that sector of the business.

Paying 40 staff in its engineering department, and running a modern design facility in Modena, meant Lamborghini was making a sizeable investment in engineering, without any immediate prospects of a return. The same applied to the extravagantly equipped headquarters of Lamborghini USA, which was failing to justify its existence because of the low sales volume.

Lamborghini USA, valued at $100,000 but with debts of $1.5m, required immediate refinancing in 1994 to meet new a US law relating to the ratio of stock market capitalisation to debt. The US authorities needed to be convinced that the company was healthy if it was to be allowed to continue trading.

The American subsidiary was renamed Automobili Lamborghini United States of America and headed by a new president, Robert A Braner, who had been part of the

Short run: inside the Diablo Roadster which went into production in 1995. Lamborghini built only 85.

"Control by a consortium in Indonesia was a massive contrast to Ferruccio's hands-on management style in the early days, but the worries turned out to be unfounded"

management team that set up the Vector Car Company. Vector claimed to make the world's fastest sports car, and so produced a direct rival to the Diablo.

Setjawan Djodi, Tommy Suharto's right-hand man, paid a visit to Sant'Agata in mid February to assess the health of Lamborghini, and to fill the vacuum left by the rapid departure of the Chrysler management. Djodi could see there was no clear business plan to replace Chrysler's vision for the manufacturer, nor a clear line of communication to headquarters in Jakarta, Indonesia's capital. Before his visit, there were concerns about Djodi and the course of action he was likely to take. Control by a consortium in Indonesia was a massive contrast to Ferruccio's hands-on management style in the early days, but the worries turned out to be unfounded. To the delight of all, Djodi rallied the support of a demoralised labour force by announcing that a new president would shortly be appointed at Sant'Agata, with a reporting line to Indonesia. A new business plan would show how Lamborghini could reach the goals that Chrysler had so optimistically set out to achieve.

The employees of Lamborghini soon warmed to Djodi, a sophisticated man aged around 50, who always dressed formally in expensive suits and loved guitar music. He assured them – via briefings to their immediate management – that the consortium was financially secure, and had money available to inject into Lamborghini. His colleagues at Sant'Agata believed him.

The backlog of Daiblos held at the factory was sold, which cleared the way for producing the new Diablo SE (Special Equipment), to be sold with a higher specification that included air conditioning, and an engine uprated to 570bhp. To avoid the complication and expense of putting the Diablo through type approval tests again, the improvements were offered as customer extras. Djodi conveyed Megatech's firm commitment to producing a small car based on the P140 and said this work would have priority in 1994. There was further news to lift the spirits: the research and development department at Sant'Agata would collaborate on the technical components of a small car to be produced in Indonesia. The package delivered by Djodi suggested that Lamborghini was about to expand as a car designer and producer, and the final cause for optimism related to the powerboat engine division. Megatech's consortium wanted product development, production and servicing to be an integral part of the factory's strategy for the next five years.

Megatech appointed agents to locate someone capable of leading Lamborghini into the second half of the 1990s. Among the applications was one from Mike Kimberley, an Englishman and once managing director of Lotus Cars, the British sports car maker. He was in charge during the time General Motors owned Lotus.

Kimberley was working for General Motors in south Asia when he heard about the opening in Italy, and applied to Megatech for the position of president of Automobili Lamborghini. He surprised one former UK Lotus dealer (by the name of David Jolliffe, who knew him well), by writing to request a reference (a favourable one was duly sent to Jakarta). News that Kimberley had been chosen brought the prospect of Lamborghini being run by someone well known in European motor industry circles.

Kimberley took charge at Sant'Agata at the end of April 1994 and soon afterwards Tommy Suharto arrived to be introduced to all as the owner (he had paid a brief discreet visit before the purchase). Suharto, accompanied by Setjawan Djodi, timed his visit to the factory to coincide with the official announcement that Megatech was the owner of Automobili Lamborghini.

Kimberley was expected to make his mark quickly, but his first action as president was a surprise. He alienated Lamborghini's predominantly Italian workforce by recruiting a team of British managers, who found homes in the Sant'Agata area. Kimberley had little faith in Italians as managers, wanted to have a team from one country who would gel and appointed people he knew he could trust.

They included Peter Stevens as technical director, an ex-Lotus engineer who was widely praised for his restyling of the Lotus Esprit Turbo. Nigel Gordon-Stewart, the international sales manager, had been brand manager at Portman, the UK Lamborghini importer. Peter Leonard-Morgan became European sales manager.

Other Italians also said they were made to feel vulnerable, including Venturelli (production manager) and Marmaroli (engineering director). Girotti, who had been running sales, Ferraris (running the accounts department) and Sandro Munari (in charge of the press office) all felt under threat, too. In fact, the whole Lamborghini workforce was left bewildered by the appointments and the direction that Kimberley seemed to want to take the company.

The only newcomer with knowledge of Lamborghini was Leonard-Morgan, who had worked with the factory for some years and understood the ethos of both the company and its cars. Predictably, he was the only one to enjoy a good working relationship with both employees and owners.

Kimberley's style of management was to remain remote from the workforce and delegate through his British managers, ignoring the culture and hands-on approach favoured in the past by Ferruccio Lamborghini, Emile Novaro and Tim Adams.

Kimberley made an early assessment of the model range, and used English consultants who, in 1994, were asked to explore the feasibility of an all-new LM002. His senior colleagues found that astonishing, considering the hard lessons already learned about the poor sales potential of such a car. In its last year of production (1992), Chrysler was able to sell only 12 of the off-roaders. Fortunately, Jakarta dropped the idea, though Kimberley always said it was Tommy Suharto who wanted to explore the possible resurrection of the LM002.

Lamborghini Engineering, which hoped again to develop Formula One engines, was not given the authority to undertake any new work for the company, and had no outside engineering contracts. On the horizon was the change in F1 rules, reducing the engine capacity from 3.5 litres to three litres, and this meant a major redesign of the V12 unit to a V10 if Lamborghini wanted to remain active in the highest level of motor racing. With no contract to sell engines to a team, Suharto decided the cost was too high. As Lamborghini Engineering was separate from Lamborghini the car manufacturer, Kimberley obtained permission from the consortium to place the company in liquidation. He proved he was as expert as founder Ferruccio in working the local laws – liquidation meant that the Court of Bologna would have to pay wages and redundancies.

Chrysler had said it owned the intellectual rights to a number of engine designs but in reality there was almost nothing when Megatech bought the business. The only exceptions were the V10 prototype and reworkings of the marine engine designs. After Kimberley appointed a liquidator, he was able to pay off Danielle Audetto, the Lamborghini Engineering general manager, and his 40 or so technicians.

Audetto's value to Lamborghini was a long list of contacts who kept him and the company up to date on technical developments. He took an executive job in superbike racing and later managed Renault's F1 team.

The liquidator tried to find someone to buy Lamborghini Engineering, but without success. There was nothing of value to buy and, eventually, sophisticated machinery was sold off at knock-down prices.

Kimberley's team discovered that Lamborghini was still owed money by several of the F1 teams that acquired its engines, but in most cases the debts were disputed, or the teams no longer existed. It is part of Lamborghini folklore that the liquidator discovered $1m/£650,000 had gone missing from a Japanese sponsor who had pledged a $3m/£2m contract.

CHAPTER 07

Sign of the times: the Diablo SV, launched in 1998, and displaying its derivative initials in flamboyant style. Lamborghini built 184.

CHAPTER 07

The liquidator is thought to have traced the money to a Monte Carlo bank account and recovered it on behalf of Lamborghini Engineering. The bank had not been instructed to pass the money to Lamborghini. Some say the liquidator recouped a further $1m/£650,000 during the disposal of Lamborghini Engineering, which in effect reduced the purchase price of the group by a useful amount.

Kimberley was intent on change but left the powerboat engine division in the capable hands of Girotti, for the big prize was won in November 1994, Megatech's first year. After several years of success in the European championships, the world championship was at last secured in the final race of the season, the Dubai Classic.

Giesse Philosophy, a boat powered by Lamborghini and piloted by Norbetto Ferretti and Luca Ferraris, took third place, which was good enough to secure the championship. Giesse Philosophy proved to be the first of a number of boats to become world champion with a Lamborghini engine and the company remains the dominant source of power, winning the 2003 championship with the Spirit of Norway.

Success on the high seas was a welcome distraction, because the delivery of promised investment into Lamborghini's bank accounts from Indonesia was somewhat erratic, and produced cashflow problems. In July 1994, there was a shift in the structure of the consortium owning Lamborghini. Megatech transferred its shares to V'Power and Sedtco, two companies effectively controlled by Tommy Suharto.

Towards the end of 1994, not enough money was going into Lamborghini to enable it to thrive, and it seemed destined to become a very low volume producer. There was concern about its ownership, because of political uncertainties in Indonesia, and the meltdown of the economies in south Asia.

The recession of the early 1990s had reduced demand for expensive cars, and it was not only Lamborghini UK that felt the pinch. During the winter of 1994/95, Porsche made an approach to take over the import concession for the UK. In view of the country's economic climate at this time, this made good business sense as operating costs could be split between the distribution structures of the two manufacturers.

This was a beneficial arrangement for both Porsche and Lamborghini as Porsche GB Ltd (a subsidiary of the German car manufacturer) was able to operate the Lamborghini Concession from the six dealerships it owned in the UK. This turned out to be a temporary arrangement and the concession was acquired by HR Owen, a London-based dealer group which also sells cars made by Volkswagen-owned Bentley in London.

Kimberley's kingdom: the British manager surprised many with the idea of bringing back LM002, but he worked local finance laws as expertly as founder Ferruccio.

Research and development on the P140 continued in 1994 but Kimberley and his team decided that designs by Gandini and Bertone (created in 1988, six years earlier) were outdated. Giorgetto Guigiaro's company, Italdesign, was commissioned to undertake a new styling exercise in late 1994 and the car was referred to as P140 Cala. The model was revealed at the 1995 Geneva motor show and gained nods of approval from the press, dealers and customers.

Yet again, when there were positive signs, Lamborghini stalled. Soon after the Geneva show, the Indonesians were shown the required level of investment needed to put the Cala into production and froze. Minimal development work continued on the only prototype, with investment going instead into the Diablo Roadster.

Turning a coupe into a convertible is difficult because removal of the roof seriously affects the car's original rigidity, and flexing of the chassis increases during high-speed cornering. This impacts on the handling and therefore also on the safety.

Marmaroli and his engineers persevered, and found a way of attaching the soft-top to the area above the engine, and behind the two occupants of the car. Through some innovative redesign, they were able to overcome the problem of flexing and the final Roadster – which gained the safety-related type approval – enjoyed better handling than the original car. By the end of 1995, Lamborghini had built only two Diablo Roadsters but in 1996 the total is thought to have been 118. Lack of certainty on production totals in a factory producing so few cars may seem odd, but it is because of the bizarre decision (presumably taken by Kimberley) to shred the archives kept by Lamborghini since its inception by Ferruccio. Stefano Pasini, whose estimates of production numbers (now counted as official) were based on sales invoices, photographs and other material, is now responsible for the Lamborghini archive which Audi has said it will protect, alongside the new museum.

The destruction of the archive was one of the actions that alienated Kimberley from his workforce at Sant'Agata. Another was his reaction to Tonino Lamborghini building a museum dedicated to the cars of his father in the grounds of Lamborghini Calor, a plant manufacturing hydraulic equipment at Dosso di Ferrara, about 10 miles from Sant'Agata. Many senior figures from the motor industry were at the opening of the museum on May 13, 1995.

Mike Kimberley declined the invitation and barred his management from attending: it was a strange and short-sighted decision as Tonino was not in competition with Sant'Agata, which had no museum of its own at that time.

Development work throughout 1995 ensured that the Diablo SV was ready to go into production in 1996, using the 5707cc Diablo engine developing 500bhp at 7000rpm. Two enthusiasts in Japan ordered a pair of special versions of the SV and these were prepared for GT racing in their country.

Marmaroli beefed up the power to 540bhp at 7100rpm but, in racing trim, the car was around 35 kilos heavier than the standard SV. The cars, designated Diablo VTR, competed with modest success in Japan and this is thought to have led Ventorelli to come up with the idea of a Lamborghini Class Challenge to be staged in 1996 and 1997. There were to be seven races, with entry restricted to the Diablo SVR and professional and amateur driver categories. The venture was shaped to raise the profile of Lamborghini, and to increase sales of the Diablo SVR.

One of the sponsors was Lease Plan France, which created a product enabling purchasers to spread their payments over two or three years, with a final payment at the end of the term to own the car outright. Lease Plan claimed that a two-year lease, allowing someone to race in the planned 1996 and 1997 championships, could cost little more than outright purchase of the car. The lease was little more than an extended payment scheme. The series proved popular and Lamborghini receive orders for 25 Diablo SVRs for the 1996 and 1997 championship, accounting for more than 10 per cent of the factory's sales for the two years. The championship was staged in Europe, and the first race was a supporting event for the 1996 Le Mans 24-hour race.

The Diablo was proving to be the all-time best-selling Lamborghini, which made the need for a strong replacement model an important priority. In 1995, when total Lamborghini sales were still sluggish, Kimberley started the process that would produce

> "For those close to Lamborghini, it was obvious that Indonesian confidence in Kimberley was waning."

that successor. He wanted something radically different and commissioned a design exercise by Zagato. The Turin studio, following severe financial problems, had re-emerged with financing by a Japanese company.

The proposed new Lamborghini was given the code number 147 and named Raptor. Development work was minimal but the Raptor – representing a break from the Lamborghini styling heritage of production models – was exhibited at the 1996 Geneva show to test the views of journalists, dealers and prospective buyers. The shape was radically different to anything previously from Lamborghini, with the exception of Flying Star, a one-off styling exercise.

While the potential of Raptor was assessed, production in 1996 was centred on the Diablo Roadster, Diablo SV and the Diablo SVR. The reconstructed archives show that 224 Diablos were built by the factory during that year. The Indonesian owners failed to match the air of optimism created at Sant'Agata by these figures and the supply of money from Indonesia became erratic. Payments to suppliers and wages were often late.

At Sant'Agata, the Italian workforce was again demoralised, and older employees felt they were part of a re-running of the Leimer era. This disillusionment was to see the departure of Franco Ferraris and, more significantly, of Luigi Marmaroli, who was hugely respected in the industry. Both found other jobs elsewhere.

Marmaroli's successor was a man of similar stature -- Massimo Ceccarani, who had been at Lamborghini since the Mimran days. He had been Marmaroli's No. 2, head of the type approval department and an innovative engineer in his own right.

For those close to Lamborghini, it was obvious that Indonesian confidence in Kimberley was waning. They needed someone they could trust to resolve the problems if the company was to have a chance to flourish in the long term.

Tommy Suharto found the right man and tempted him out of retirement. Vittorio Di Capua had worked for Fiat for 40 years and running the group's UK distribution company and managing Ferrari America were among his roles.

Di Capua was appointed joint president (Kimberley was demoted to similar status) and delved into the company's finances and resources. The Italian was unhappy with some aspects of the accounts prepared by Kimberley. There was a heated exchange between the two men who failed to reach an agreement on Lamborghini's financial position.

It was then a question of which joint vice president of Lamborghini convinced Suharto and his colleagues in Jakarta. In November 1996, the Indonesians accepted the figures prepared by Di Capua, which was hardly surprising as they had appointed him to do the financial detective work. This made Kimberley's position untenable and he left Lamborghini in the same month.

Di Capua was now sole president and within two months the English contingent had left the factory. The new boss had to recruit his own management team to head the sales, accounts, public relations, production, marine engine and other departments. This was a major undertaking, given the fragile perception of Lamborghini in the eyes of many automotive industry executives at the time.

Gianfranco Ventorelli, the head of production engineering design, was next to leave amid discussions about the way orders for spare parts were placed. Sandro Munari, the head of public relations, opted to quit because he did not see a suitable role for himself under the new regime.

Ceccarani's engineering department was expanded to take over production and development. Giuseppi Girotti, Sgarzi's successor as Lamborghini's sales director, was suffering from ill health and retired in December 1996, at about the same time as the closure of the Bugatti plant at nearby Compogalliano. Ferruccio had been a close friend of the owner of Bugatti, whose cars were largely engineered by former Lamborghini employees. Volkswagen was to acquire Bugatti, placing it alongside Lamborghini and Bentley as valuable historic marques with potential for development.

At the start of 1997, Lamborghini's day-to-day management was secure in the hands of Di Capua but the outlook continued to be uncertain. Economies in the Far East were close to collapse, and the position in Indonesia was even more acute, because the political position of President Suharto was so insecure. Suharto eventually resigned in May 1998 after weeks of mounting opposition to his rule and 32 years in power. During 1997, Tommy Suharto was seldom seen at Sant'Agata and this contributed to a feeling the company was gradually becoming distant from its owners.

Di Capua focused on producing accounts that reflected the true position of Lamborghini. The company was experiencing constant cash flow problems, causing rumours about its ability to survive to spread among suppliers, staff and customers.

The balance sheet for 1996 showed that Lamborghini's assets – primarily manufacturing plant, other buildings and cars – were worth about $88m/£59m. The corresponding figure for 1997, up to July of that year, was only $11m/£6.8m.

It meant that Lamborghini's value was dangerously low and Di Capua had to act quickly before concern started to be expressed about the viability of the company. He secured loans and a capital injection from Indonesian Timor Car (which manufactured and sold vehicles in its own country) to increase Lamborghini's balance sheet to $30m/£18.75m.

Timor, in which the Suharto family were shareholders, gained a stake in Lamborghini. The Indonesian company was seemingly unaware of the saga of the disastrous LM002 because it decided it wanted to develop an off-road vehicle that would use some components designed by Lamborghini.

Timor's investment produced some breathing space for Di Capua but he recognised the need to slash the factory's overheads. This he was able to achieve by vigorous cost cutting and a reduction in the labour force from 500 people to around 400, mainly through wastage and redundancy.

Lamborghini built and sold 216 Diablos in 1997 and on a factory turnover of $13m/£7.8m Di Cappua was able to report a modest profit, whereas the company had lost money the previous year while selling approximately the same number of cars.

Di Capua also decided it was time to resolve the problem of ALUSA (Automobili Lamborghini USA), the company's import centre in Florida, which was accumulating massive trading losses. The American invoices were building up at ALUSA and Sant'Agata.

Lamborghini's president could not see a way of making the venture profitable and, strapped for cash at the factory, he decided to stop shipping cars to ALUSA, and so avoid further losses in America.

At the Detroit auto show in January 1998, Lamborghini announced the termination of its US distribution concession held by ALUSA. The new distributor was Vic Keuylian, the head of a multi-franchise retail car company called Excellent, and an experienced Lamborghini dealer. Excellent was financially strong and bought the 30 or so American specification Diablos held by ALUSA.

The deal eased Di Capua's cash flow problems and reopened the prospect of selling Lamborghinis in America which remained a potentially valuable market.

May 1998 marked the 35th anniversary of Lamborghini and something was needed to restore confidence in the company among customers (existing, and new) and dealers. During 1997, the design of the P147 Raptor was changed by Zagato and its Japanese styling partner, Nori Harada. The revamped and repainted car was presented to Lamborghini during the anniversary celebrations at the factory. The reaction of Lamborghini management, customers and dealers was mixed.

High priority: success for the Diablo brought investment for the Roadster at the expense of the P140 Cala prototype.

Criticism was based on a shape that lacked the aggressive look of the Diablo, and some felt it did not represent the traditional aesthetics of a top-of-the-range Lamborghini.

How Lamborghini was missing the confidence of its founder – Ferruccio had passionate views about design, and carried all with him. Now the company was struggling to clamber out of a troubled period, lacking direction and adequate investment.

Some of the Lamborghini management wanted to go ahead with production but the project was effectively scrapped in June 1998.

The research and development cost of the Raptor totalled some $37m£22.5m – money

> "Di Capua was using his experience and contacts to try to secure a much more realistic collaboration with a major car manufacturer. During 1997, he made the first approach to Audi"

spent on a car that never made it to the production area. This made the prototype Raptor a hot property, and it became the property of Alain Wikki, a Swiss investor in Zagato. The details of the transaction remained confidential, and it is not known whether Wikki bought the car, or was given it in partial compensation of the money he had lost in the development of Raptor. In 2000, the car was sold at auction by Brooks of Geneva for $216,000/£149,000. It was thought to have been bought by a wealthy man from Japan, who was either a Lamborghini enthusiast, or who saw a good investment.

Rumours were rife at Sant'Agata in 1998 and the most worrying was that the Indonesian owners might move production out of Italy. Indonesia was seen as one possibility, and Lamborghini had the link with Timor through the development of a 4x4 known at Sant'Agata as the Borneo. Tommy Suharto, as a shareholder in Lamborghini and Timor, seemed to favour the idea, and there were potential cost-saving and other benefits.

Suharto wanted Timor's image to be enhanced by using a Lamborghini-designed engine, and the project would have created additional work for the design team at Sant'Agata. The theory was fine, but the reality always appeared highly unlikely, and the project was scrapped in 1997. This also laid to rest the ominous notion that Lamborghini production might be uprooted from Italy, and moved to Indonesia.

Di Capua was using his experience and contacts to try to secure a much more realistic collaboration with a major car manufacturer. During 1997, he made the first approach to Audi, part of the mighty Volkswagen Group.

There were reasons for believing Audi could be interested in some form of collaboration between the two companies. Lamborghini had designed and built exotic sports cars for more than 35 years, and through LM002 demonstrated an interest in 4x4.

Audi's commitment to manufacturing performance cars had taken on new meaning in March 1980, when it unveiled the Quattro at the Geneva motor show. The coupe was the first high-performance car with four-wheel drive, and in time the quattro system was to be used throughout the Audi range.

Di Capua's initial approach to Audi in 1997 was to discuss the use of its V8 engine and Quattro system in the P140 – the car known as the 'baby Lambo'. The talks left Di Capua feeling optimistic but hard negotiations remained.

Other collaborations were pursued in 1997. Lamborghini started to negotiate to build a design by Norbo Nakamura, the Japanese designer. Nakamura's car, the Aerosa, was powered by Ford's 4.8-litre V8 Mustang engine, and the idea was that it would be developed and manufactured by Lamborghini. Sales were running well below Sant'Agata's production capacity, which increased the cost per unit.

The Aerosa was exhibited at the 1997 Geneva show, a venue regarded by Lamborghini as the historical home of its new models, but this car was presented as a product of Gigliato Design, founded by Nakamura.

The idea was that Lamborghini would construct the cars, using major components supplied by Ford, and supply them to Gigliato Design, which would sell them either directly to buyers, or via dealers. The retail price was to be around $65,000/£39,000. Norbo Nokamura was convinced the Aerosa would take sales from the Ferrari 355 and considerably undercut the price of cars in its market sector.

It was, though, difficult to see how Lamborghini could finance the development of the car, invest in production facilities to build it and still make a profit in view of the projected retail price. Nokamura wanted to finalise an agreement with his Gigliato Design in time for production to start in 1999. The agreement was never formally completed and this became another Lamborghini project that failed to materialise.

In the final months of Lamborghini under Indonesian ownership, there was yet another twist to the story. Vector, the US supercar manufacturer founded by Jerry Wiegert, had in the late 1980s been acquired by V'Power, part of the consortium that bought Lamborghini.

V'Power closed Vector in 1996 and it was acquired two years later by American Dream International. When production started again in 1998, Lamborghini was supplying its V12 5707cc, 500bhp Diablo engine to power the Vector M12. Fantastic performance figures were claimed and Lamborghini's input was duly praised.

The Vector M12 was road tested by Jeremy Clarkson, presenter of BBC TV's *Top Gear* programme in the UK. Clarkson's forthright comments built the programme's popularity, which in turn made it highly influential. He made a comment about the Vector which went along the lines of 'rubbish with a gem of an engine'. This savaging of the Vector, when assessed alongside negative comments in magazines and newspapers, motivated Di Capua to stop supplying Lamborghini engines to Vector.

Di Capua was becoming much more careful - this was the man who, in 1997, is believed to have approached Romano Artioli, the man behind the renaissance of Bugatti, now also part of Volkswagen group.

The reason for Di Capua's determination to take special care of Lamborghini's image was the continuing, top secret negotations with Audi. This was now receiving the attention of Ferdinand Piëch, chairman of the Volkswagen Group, which included Audi. The former head of Porsche's endurance racing programme was an admirer of Lamborghini's cars and recognised the skills that existed at Sant'Agata.

Piëch felt that a marriage was possible between those skills and the solidity and strength of Audi. Slowly a dialogue started between the two companies, with a view to Audi acquiring Lamborghini. Initially these were difficult, partly because of language difficulties between the Indonesians and the German giant. Tommy Suharto spoke English but usually had an entourage of business associates who did not. The differences in business practice between Europe and south Asia was a further complication.

The Indonesians put their faith in Di Capua to broker a deal and, on June 12, 1998, the two sides signed a heads of agreement document, for the sale of Lamborghini to Audi. Volkswagen group accountants and other specialists were given access to Lamborghini's records to ensure there were no hidden debts or other problems.

Di Capua had done his job in putting everything straight and, on August 4, 1998, Audi agreed to buy Lamborghini. The sum paid to Megatech is the subject of a confidentiality clause but is believed to be around $18m/£11.25m. Lamborghini was about to start another period in its turbulent history. Enthusiasts around the globe wondered how tiny Lamborghini would fare as a business within the powerful Audi business, itself a division of the Volkswagen group. And how a tiny maker of Italian super sports cars – that had almost lost its identity as a procession of owners failed to make it a lasting success – could retain its identity as part of one of the leading multi-national car manufacturers.

"Between 1998 and 2003, during the vital first five years of Audi stewardship, Lamborghini flourished while Chrysler continued to struggle as part of DaimlerChrysler"

08_Audi partner! Four new rings for the fighting bull

Even Lamborghini loyalists who yearned for a miraculous return to the pioneering days when Ferruccio guided the marque by passion and instinct were confident that Audi would be, at the very least, a caring owner with long-term ambitions. The depth of engineering experience, and the extent of its facilities, would also create confidence at Sant'Agata.

Between 1998 and 2003, during the vital first five years of Audi stewardship, Lamborghini flourished while Chrysler continued to struggle as part of DaimlerChrysler.

The US corporation, on acquiring Lamborghini, had described it as 'the jewel in Chrysler's crown' and promised much, though failed to deliver. By the end the 1990s, the fault lines in Chrysler that had led to problems with Lamborghini were fully exposed.

In 1998, Chrysler and Daimler-Benz announced a merger and Chrysler's executives proclaimed it as a 'marriage made in heaven'. That year, Megatech sold Lamborghini to Audi.

Business journalists who wrote at the time about the creation of DaimlerChrysler said

Across borders: Gallardo, developed with the aid of German engineering expertise, takes to the road in its native Italy.

CHAPTER 08

it was more a take-over by Daimler-Benz than a merger. Either way, it meant that Lamborghini and Chrysler came to be controlled by the two German giants of the automotive industry.

Chrysler's experience continued to be uncomfortable, with the closure of many manufacturing plants, and job losses totalling around 63,000. The DaimlerChrysler business plan was intended to return Chrysler to making an operating profit by the end of 2003 (which it didn't) -- Audi had a similar ambition for Lamborghini, and achieved it. Audi gained Lamborghini during the summer of 1998.

Megatech and Audi signed a letter of intent on June 2 and the final agreement was signed on July 24. The deal was completed on August 4 and the Volkswagen group laid out its plans.

Racing reality: Ferruccio always resisted motorsport but, under Audi, Lamborghini developed a competitive version of the Diablo GTR *(right and far right)*.

Audi produced investment as promised, kept a tight management grip on the new facilities and provided assurances about a new model plan. Customers, dealers and the workforce all responded positively. Even so, given the state of Sant'Agata, it was a remarkable turnabout, and cause for celebration among a workforce that had endured the depressing final years of Chrysler's reign, and the uncertainty of the Megatech era.

Audi began with a number of simple objectives. First, it conducted a rigorous examination of Lamborghini's facilities, models under development and the skill of the workforce. Secondly, Audi knew that previous owners had been correct to judge that Sant'Agata needed to build and sell a minimum of 1,500 cars a year to be viable. Those cars had to be of the highest quality to justify their purchase price, and have a special

Solo model: Lamborghini was building only the Diablo SV *(above and above right)* and its derivative, the SLR, when Audi acquired the company.

appeal that would bring pride to Lamborghini ownership.

It was also clear to Audi that selling 30 Lamborghinis a week could not be achieved with only a top-of-the-range replacement for the Diablo. A so-called 'baby Diablo' was essential to make the business plan viable, and Audi insisted that the smaller car had to be ready for sale within two years of completing the design of the new flagship model.

Profitable car-making was the most important objective of Lamborghini Holdings Spa, the new subsidiary formed by Audi in 1998, but not the only one. In addition to the car-making Automobili Lamborghini Spa, Dr Ferdinand Piëch and his Audi board colleagues also entrusted to the group control of Motori Marini Spa (the new name for the powerboat engine division), Lamborghini Artimarca (a licensing and merchandising company) and

Autogerma, the Volkswagen group distributor for Italy.

Autogerma is a substantial business, which in 2003 imported into Italy 280,000 vehicles across Volkswagen's four non-specialist brands – VW, Audi, SEAT and Skoda. It is operated as a separate business but there are tax advantages for Volkswagen, which can offset some of the tax liabilities of the distributor's profits against the investment going into Lamborghini.

On Audi Day 1, Lamborghini employed 450 people and this had risen to 650 by January 2004. Extra engineers were recruited to strengthen the research and development department. Support from Audi was set up, with senior Lamborghini engineers and other key staff given a close working relationship with their opposite number at Audi.

Rodolfo Rocchio, a senior Audi executive, was appointed chairman of Lamborghini, knowing that the group would come under the close scrutiny of Dr Piëch, chairman of both Volkswagen group and Audi.

Rocchio made a good start, and was welcomed as Lamborghini's saviour. He invited the popular Vittorio Di Capua to continue as chief executive officer of Automobili Lamborghini, with Massimo Ceccarani remaining head of engineering.

Audi's review of Sant'Agata included an assessment of floor space, quality control and other key aspects of production. Existing and future car models, production facilities and research and development were examined in detail.

At that time, Lamborghini was producing only the Diablo SV (including a few SV roadsters) and its derivative, the SLR. The only new model under development was the Zagato Raptor, and Audi was quick to recognise the urgency of preparing a replacement

137

CHAPTER 08

Sant'Agata today: Ferruccio's factory has been transformed, with heavy investment by Audi in developing and producing cars, and a museum to promote Lamborghini *(right)*.

Designer cars: Walter de' Silva, left (Audi group head of design) and Luc Donckerwolke *(far right)*, made responsible for Lamborghini design in 2003, with a Murciélago.

for Diablo. This challenge was similar to Chrysler's need to replace the Countach on its acquisition of Lamborghini in 1987.

In 1998, Lamborghini built 213 cars, less than an sixth of the annual 1,500 seen by Audi as break-even point. It did not take the experienced Audi management long to work out that the Raptor was nowhere near ready for a motor show because it could not be

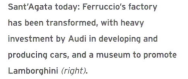

138

presented as a pre-production model. Piëch ordered work on the Raptor to end and this came as a surprise to few, as the Volkswagen group boss was expected to want the next Lamborghini to have Audi's influence in it from the outset of development. The project was allocated the tight deadline of two years, with the research and development department given the additional burden of producing new derivatives of existing models to provide a platform for future Lamborghini expansion.

Piëch did not scrap the Raptor design entirely. Audi decided to retain the chassis, engine and transmission developed by Ceccarani and his department, which meant that something of the soul of 'old Lamborghini' would continue into the next generation.

Outside stylists and coachbuilding companies wanted to work with a reinvigorated Lamborghini and collaboration with Bertone was restored, though without the close bonding that had led to the creation of the Miura.

In September 1998, Audi appointed its own design coordinator at Lamborghini. Luc Donckerwolke, a Belgian citizen born in Peru, joined Audi Design as a stylist in 1992 at its

Farewell to Diablo: the last model known as the 6-litre was produced for two years while its successor was developed *(above and right)*

base in Ingolstadt after starting as a designer with Peugeot in France. From 1994-96, he worked for Skoda (like Audi, part of the Volkswagen group) in the Czech Republic, before returning to Germany to become responsible for Audi concept development.

Cars bearing Donckerwolfe's styling signature had included the Audi A4 Avant and R8 Le Mans, and the Skoda Octavia and Fabia, by the time he moved to Sant'Agata. He relished the design challenge of keeping faith with the shape of Lamborghini, while

"In September 1998, a revised version of the P147 Raptor concept was ready to go before the Audi board"

developing a fresh look. His first task was to revise the styling of Diablo for the definitive version, powered by the Lamborghini V12, which had been enlarged to six litres by Ceccarani's department.

In September 1998, a revised version of the P147 Raptor concept was ready to go before the Audi board, and it was given the go-ahead, though some at Lamborghini (including Di Capua) continued to believe the original 147 would have been successful.

Donckerwolke and his team now had two years to bring together a car with a new shape and existing engine, gearbox and other major components. The prototype was code-numbered 147/2.

By late 1998, Audi/Lamborghini had completed its survey of Sant'Agata and created a design for additional facilities. The following year, more land was purchased and work started on a new administrative block, a Lamborghini motor museum and a car showroom.

Audi gave employees a chance to settle to the new ownership before making management changes at Lamborghini in 1999. It was time for Vittorio Di Capua to retire after leading Automobili Lamborghini through a bruising time during the Megatech ownership.

CHAPTER 08

Into his place stepped Giuseppe Greco in the joint role of vice chairman of the Board and managing director, and he was ideally qualified for the job. He was hugely experienced, with nearly 40 years at Fiat Auto behind him, which meant he was familiar with the way large groups operated.

The bonus was that Greco had been Ferrari's general manager in the USA, Canada and Switzerland for Fiat, and so had intimate knowledge of Lamborghini's great rival. He was lured to Sant'Agata by Audi's ambitions and did not disappoint, marrying its rigorous requirements in terms of quality control and efficiency with the natural flair of the Lamborghini workforce. He was instrumental in forging goodwill and a spirit of collaboration between equivalent staff at Lamborghini and Audi.

The first full year of Audi ownership meant that Lamborghini was the centre of frenetic activity throughout 1999. The German group quickly demonstrated its enthusiasm and thoroughness and pushed ahead with the improvement of existing models, and the development of a new range.

A few years earlier, Chrysler had produced the Anniversary Countach as a stopgap model to retain interest in the marque while research and development pushed ahead with a replacement. Now, Audi was overseeing a final version of the Diablo.

Donckerwolke rapidly stamped his authority on the design of the Diablo replacement and the pace of the work quickened. Collaboration with Bertone and other outside stylists was terminated so that Audi's man and his in-house team were entirely responsible for the car that would materialise, with Audi styling guru Walter De' Silva holding a watching brief on the programme from a distance.

Donckerwolke had refined the front of the Diablo 6-litre and the work on the nose was carried over to the new car. He wanted to radically restyle the model from the cockpit to the rear, make it slimmer and more stylish and retain the heritage of Lamborghini by including features such as the flamboyant spider door that swung upwards when opened.

To help him to achieve these objectives, Massimo Ceccarani's department came up with a smaller power unit, reducing its height by using a dry-sump lubrication system. This gave the car a lower centre of gravity which in turn improved the handling.

The trusted V12 engine, with 60-degree angle, was retained and the capacity increased to 6192cc, producing 500bhp at 7500rpm. The engine was married to a six-speed gearbox developed and built at Sant'Agata. Performance was to be sharpened by a new fuel injection system and safety improved through the latest ABS anti-lock brakes.

"Audi made the most of the marketing opportunity that arose from the end of production of Lamborghini's biggest-selling model,"

The final Diablo, to be known as the 6-litre, was produced for only 24 months, the time allowed for the development of its successor. Its most important feature was four-wheel-drive which was Lamborghini's own, because Audi agreed this was better for the car than its own Quattro system.

Audi viewed two changes as essential, ruling that the GT had become over burdened with air ducts, which had evolved as the norm on high-speed supercars to cool the oil and water through the whole performance range. This had been resolved on the GT and the GTR with the introduction of air boxes on the roof leading to the engine compartment.

Donckerwolke tidied up the styling of the Diablo, smoothing the aerodynamics around the nose area. The 6-litre Diablo used Lamborghini's V12 Quattrovalve 5992cc engine with power reduced to 550bhp at 7300rpm to make the car more driveable. The weight increased to 1625kgs but, with the smoother nose, top speed was around 200 mph.

The first Diablo to be marketed under the new ownership was the GT announced in 1999. This retained the V12 60-degree Quattrovalvole engine, producing 575bhp. Lamborghini offered a variety of gear ratios and rear wing configurations to customers. These options marginally affected the top speed but increased acceleration and handling. Following the model's debut in 1999 at the Frankfurt motor show, Lamborghini built around 80 of the cars during that and the following year.

Motor racing, always opposed by Ferruccio, was becoming a reality. Lamborghini developed a special version of the Diablo GTR for a racing championship restricted to this model. It was also to compete in GT endurance racing.

The power of the GTR was increased from the V12 5992 cc engine to 509bhp at 7300 revs.

The GT's weight was reduced from 1490kgs to 1400kgs, and in standard race trim the car was geared with a top speed of 212 mph.

The GTR was raced in Europe, the USA and Australia with sales totalling around 30 cars. During 1999, Lamborghini also sold the Diablo SV Roadster, which was produced to special order – this marked the end of targa top production.

The 6-litre Diablo, sold only with metallic gold paintwork and black leather interior, made its debut at the Geneva show in the spring of 2000 and went into production in the same year, with Sant'Agata building the car until July 2001. Orders flowed in throughout that period and 383 cars were built.

Audi made the most of the marketing opportunity that arose from the end of production of Lamborghini's biggest-selling model, and the final 50 cars were marketed as

Team effort: engineers at Lamborghini were assisted by all departments at Audi to put the Murciélago *(above and right)* into production in 2003.

Remembering Ferruccio: Lamborghini built 50 Murciélago 40th Anniversary models *(above and right)* and 250 owners' cars travelled in procession to the founder's birthplace.

a limited edition Diablo 6 litre SE. Lamborghini enthusiasts regarded the car as a fitting climax to 11 years production of Diablo.

The number of Diablos built is a matter of debate because Megatech shredded the Lamborghini archives. The guide to the company's museum puts the figure at 2,903 but the total is thought to be nearer 3,300.

In early 2000, Lamborghini froze the design of the new car that was later to be announced as the Murciélago. It was the product of intensive work at Sant'Agata combined with technical contributions from elsewhere in Audi. Those aware of the car were confident about its potential.

Construction of the first prototype body was contracted out to two engineering companies in Turin, Tesco and ATR, and the first complete bodyshell and chassis reached Sant'Agata in June 2000.

By the end of the same month, the development team at Sant'Agata had fitted the engine, transmission, suspension and other mechanical components, and a running prototype of the car that was to replace Diablo was ready for testing.

Its first challenge was scrutiny by the demanding members of the board of Audi Neustadt, the company's technical centre in Germany, in early July.

Approval for production was granted, sales volumes estimated and a budget agreed. October of the following year, 2001, was set as the latest for delivery of the first cars. The Murciélago was to have a tubular steel chassis (the only major unit from an outside

CHAPTER 08

supplier) clad with body panels comprising carbon fibre units manufactured at Sant'Agata. A steel roof panel was added make the model more rigid.

The name chosen for Audi's first Lamborghini was true to the tradition started by Ferruccio, and it was to honour another fighting bull. Murciélago was spared at the end of a bullfight in 1879 as a tribute to its strength and courage.

The bull was given to the breeder Don Miura (whose surname was, of course, also used by Lamborghini) and went on to father a formidable line of fighting bulls that extends to the present day. The benefit to Lamborghini of being part of a large group was further emphasised when Audi authorised the production of eight prototypes: Murciélago had to be right.

The cars were used for extensive road testing in several countries, crash testing and gaining type approval the USA, Europe, Switzerland (which is outside the EU) and Japan. Most Lamborghinis are sold in 20 countries, with the USA being the best market. It takes around 35% of production, followed by Germany (18%) and the UK (10%). The technical department at Sant'Agata had to ensure the Murciélago complied with emissions limits and other requirements in all its markets

During 2000, Audi carried out a reappraisal of the 'baby Diablo' project (the car would be Gallardo), which included Marmaroli's V10 and a succession of styling exercises. All but Italdesign's Giuglaro-styled concept were abandoned.

Luc Donckerwolke and Lamborghini Centro Stile (central styling) worked with Audi Engineering which decided the car needed a new engine and transmission. Audi decided to stick with a V10 but with a 90-degree angle. This would lower the position of the power unit and that was essential because of Audi's styling plans for the car.

Bench testing was started in 2001, with the factory developing a new six-speed gearbox. Audi was bullish about the 'baby Diablo', planning 2,000 sales a year, which made strong marketing essential. The model was to take Lamborghini into a new area of the sports car market.

Motoring magazines started to pick up bits of information about the car and pressed the factory for more details. Audi welcomed the speculation, because it whetted the appetite of prospective buyers, but the moment soon came when it was necessary to give the car a name.

All Spain's fighting bulls are descended from five species, and one of them is called Gallardo, the name chosen by Audi. Announcing the name meant that Lamborghini could encourage people to discard the term 'baby Diablo' which was a double misnomer. The car

Bright prospect: Audi saw that Gallardo *(right)*, **if successful, could take factory production over 1,000 units a year for the first time.**

CHAPTER 08

Name change: Lamborghini made an early announcement about Gallardo *(right, far right and overleaf)* **to discourage use of the description 'baby Diablo'.**

was not a Diablo and, though smaller than Murciélago, was hardly a 'baby'.

Gallardo was to be powered by a V10 double overhead camshaft, four-valve V90 5-litre 500bhp engine with a top speed of over 300kph (more than 185mph). To most other motor manufacturers, this would be a top-of-the-range supercar.

For Gallardo, Audi chose a spaceframe clad with body panels, all made from aluminium, to be made at Audi Neckarsulm, one of the world's leading specialists in producing composite aluminium for cars. The Gallardo in some ways represented the most important model in Lamborghini history: if successful it would see the factory production exceed 1,000 units a year for the first time and bring a return on Audi's investment.

Styling the Gallardo represented few problems because many features had been worked out during the development of the Murciélago. The permanent four-wheel drive and other mechanical features were all familiar territory for Lamborghini. Audi gave approval in 2001 for the Gallardo to enter production in 2003. Painted body shells and chassis were to be completed at Neckarsulm and transported to Sant'Agata for assembly.

Leading motoring journalists from around the world flew to Italy in September 2001 for the international press launch of the Murciélago at Sant'Agata and Bologna. Many owners with their cars, and Lamborghini dealers with their clients, also arrived to preview the successor to Miura, Countach and Diablo. The Murciélago was to receive generous praise for its performance, handling, styling and – most importantly – build quality.

The retirement in 2001 of Ferdinand Piëch as chairman of Volkswagen group created a management change for Lamborghini. Piëch's replacement as chairman of Audi and Lamborghini Holdings Spa was Walter Winterkorn, Audi's technical director.

His appointment underlined Audi's commitment to Lamborghini which, through the development of the Murciélago, had been totally integrated into the German group, while keeping its distinctive and separate identity.

The first phase of Audi's development of the Sant'Agata site was completed in 2001,

with the opening of the museum and administration accommodation on what had been a staff car park. The new two-storey structure was clad in tinted glass to make a design statement in keeping with the quality of the cars being produced nearby.

The Gallardo production line was installed between September 2002 and February 2003, and the first car went to the Geneva motor show in the March for its world debut. Within a few months, Lamborghini's dealers had committed themselves to buying all the Gallardos to be built in 2003/04. To the delight of Audi, the American retail network was the quickest to place orders, and this accounted for 35% of the cars to be built.

From April to December 2003, Lamborghini production was running on double shifts, producing 890 Gallardos. In the year as a whole, Lamborghini, built 415 Murciélagos to make a total output of vehicles of 1,305. A return to profitability finally seemed secure for Lamborghini after 12 years operating at a loss.

The restructuring of the plant was completed by spring 2003, in time for the launch of the Gallardo. The facilities included a new building for Centro Stile, Lamborghini's first fully-equipped styling studio. That year, Luc Donckerwolke was rewarded for his design work on Murciélago and Gallardo and appointed head of design at Lamborghini, reporting to Walter de' Silva, Audi group head of design.

Sant'Agata also has a new research and development department, there have been major changes to the aftersales department and employees use a new canteen facility.

This activity brought a satisfactory conclusion to the first four decades of Lamborghini as a car manufacturer. Lamborghini marked the occasion by building 50 Murciélago 40th Anniversary models, all painted jade green. In October 2003, members of Lamborghini Clubs worldwide were invited to Sant'Agata to celebrate the anniversary.

Around 250 Lamborghinis were at the event, which included a procession to Renazzo, the birthplace of Ferruccio Lamborghini. It was a fitting tribute to the founder a car company which seemed, at long last, to have found success again after appearing to be close to disaster for so many years.

For Audi, the start of Lamborghini's fifth decade brought the need to address the future and to consider how the model line-up would be replaced over the next 10 years. Audi had laid the foundations: now it needed to maximise its investment.

"A large crowd of journalists from around the world witnessed the spectacular introduction of the Murciélago Roadster"

09_Bullish on the future; back to fighting form

In early March 2004, on press day at the Geneva motor show, the tall black wall at the back of the Lamborghini stand parted to reveal a car pointing to the heavens. It was somehow symbolic of the manufacturer's ambitions, five years into the Audi era and 40 years after Ferruccio started building supercars.

To the backdrop of flashing lights and upbeat music, a large crowd of journalists from around the world witnessed the spectacular introduction of the Murciélago Roadster, the third model to be seen since the German group took command in 1998.

Manufacturers are allocated slots of 15 minutes or so for their introductions on international motor show press days and there is intense competition for the time of influential journalists. The model had already been seen as a concept car at the 2003 Detroit show but Lamborghini has always created excitement, especially with a first glimpse of a production convertible.

The chopped-top Murciélago did not disappoint and journalists were able to sit in and

On the grid: the Murciélago R-GT, unveiled at the 2003 Frankfurt motor show and for sale to anyone competing in the GT or American Le Mans series.

CHAPTER 09

inspect the horizontal Roadster on the stand.

Lamborghini was confident the resulting press coverage would create a strong global demand for the model before production began in the second half of 2004.

Away from the spotlights on the same day, its executives were answering searching questions about the future for the Murciélago coupe, because it was more expensive than the smaller but similar Gallardo. Leading international automotive journalists were interested in how Audi would shape the model range of its prized marque up to and beyond 2010.

Widening the Lamborghini choice, while giving additional depth through specialist derivatives, has been Audi's objective since it bought Lamborghini.

With Murciélago and Gallardo as the only offerings, it was up to Luc Donckerwolke, Lamborghini's head of design, to make the Roadster more than just a soft-top version of the Murciélago coupe that arrived in 2003. Lamborghini wanted three distinct models on sale at the end of 2004 and marketing material handed to journalists at Geneva spoke of the Murciélago Roadster as "a truly unique model". In reality, it is a convertible version of a coupe, though with some imaginative styling changes.

The model continues Lamborghini's 12-cylinder roadster tradition, from the 350 GTS through the Miura to the Diablo.

Donckerwolke was driven to make the cabin "more extreme and exclusive" than ever, he said. The driver's side has different material to the passenger's, and is perforated, which was intended to accentuate the pleasure of being at the wheel. Streamlined headrests for both occupants are equipped with mobile air vents and new exhausts have a more aggressive look than those of the Murciélago Coupe. The Roadster had much to catch the eye but magazine journalists were saying that Lamborghini still has much to achieve.

Angus MacKenzie, editor of the UK's *Car* magazine, believes Gallardo's performance and price means the whole Murciélago concept needs rethinking. "One scenario is to replace it with an even more awesome supercar capable of taking on the Ferrari Enzo," said MacKenzie after the Roadster debut in 2004.

"Such a vehicle would probably share its structure with the Gallardo and boast an all-new V12 derived from the Audi-engineered V8/V10 engine. Or Lamborghini could look at a powerful front-engined 2+2 modelled along the lines of the memorable Espada coupe."

Lamborghini's ambitions for Gallardo include a rear-wheel drive competition version (a

"Executives were answering searching questions about the future for the Murciélago coupe"

Moving up: Lamborghini widened its range by launching the Murciélago Roadster at the 2004 Geneva motor show.

rival for the Porsche 911 GT2) in 2004, a soft-top Barchetta in 2005 and higher-performance 550bhp GT in 2007.

Longer-term, according to *Car*, there is a genuine third model – an all-roader, but far removed from the disastrous LM002. This long-term project, aimed at 2010-2012, is believed to be a lightweight spaceframe crossover, with the emphasis on agility and fuel efficiency.

Lamborghini's immediate challenge is the commercial success of the Murciélago Roadster, the most recent fruit of Audi investment totalling 350m euros (approximately $390m/£245m).

This has been directed both into developing future models and enhancing the technology in the current range. At the Frankfurt motor show in the autumn of 2003, Lamborghini introduced e-gear as an option on both Murciélago and Gallardo. This is a gearbox with an electronically-controlled sequential shifting system which gives the driver manual control of ratio changes without a clutch pedal.

Similar systems have been offered by other manufacturers for some time, and it was an example of Audi investing to bring Lamborghini up to date in a way that was essential for planned future growth.

Under Audi's stewardship, Lamborghini turnover increased five-fold from 40m euros (about $45m/£28m) in 1999 to 200m euros ($225m/£140m) in 2003. Further growth of between 20 and 30 per cent is expected by 2009.

Between 1999 and 2003, Lamborghini's workforce increased from just under 300 to about 750 employees. This is large enough for the current production capacity but would rise by around 50 if Lamborghini felt it could justify a second shift on the Gallardo assembly line.

Giueseppe Greco, Lamborghini's vice chairman and chief executive officer, talked in spring 2004 about the company's ambitions and the balance between past and future. He acknowledged that the first 40 years were "quite bumpy", and said there was rarely an owner of the company capable of developing a product strategy with the resources to carry it through.

"With the Audi purchase, we have entered a new and more structured phase of our life as a company," he said. "For the first time we are in a position to have a number of fundamental positive factors working for our success.

"Audi has the financial strength to sustain a heavy investment commitment, and to

> "Being part of the bigger family has broadened our vision and our ambitions and given us the chance to find out how much of our original culture was worth preserving."
>
> **Giuseppe Greco, Lamborghini's vice chairman and chief executive officer**

give Lamborghini two new product lines and the production capacity to assure a dynamic growth strategy.

"As part of the biggest automotive group in Europe, we have access to component suppliers that, in the past, were not so keen to produce components for such a small company. This will dramatically improve our product quality and give our customers more value for their money.

"We have now access to all group infrastructures (such as testing grounds, wind tunnels and laboratories) and the intelligence and professionalism of a number of Audi experts who, with real car-nut enthusiasm, are helping us solve all engineering and production problems.

"Being part of the bigger family has broadened our vision and our ambitions and given us the chance to find out how much of our original culture was worth preserving. We discovered which parts had to be changed, either because they were technologically obsolete or stemmed from a past of low ambitions caused by lack of resources."

Greco and the other board members are acutely aware of a new challenge emerging for Lamborghini and its great rival Ferrari: volume manufacturers are seeking a slice of the global performance car market. This raises a question about the strength of the Lamborghini brand in the eyes of a new generation of potential owners.

"The expected growth of the numbers of people who would be financially capable of purchasing this type of vehicle, with the baby-boomer generation turning 50, has encouraged many new entries who have announced projects to build or develop performance cars.

"Naturally the motivations are different. For manufacturers such as Lamborghini and Ferrari, this product concept is the core business of the company; for others this could be a good profit opportunity or, at the very least, an image-building initiative."

Greco hopes that growth in competitive mature markets, and the opening of new potential in countries such as China and India (and some in eastern Europe - will benefit both Lamborghini and the non-traditional supercar manufacturers.

"The problem, paradoxically, will be the increased choice that the consumer will have, and the 'fashion effect' of numerous new entries year after year," he said. "It will be difficult to ensure a product lifecycle without continuous updates and restyling, thus making the economics of this market segment more and more challenging.

"In this complex landscape, I think that Lamborghini will have an important role to play

Ready for action: with the Murciélago Roadster *(above)* and future models, Lamborghini is preparing to face a challenge from new entrants to the supercar market.

In the lead: the Murciélago R-GT *(right)* set the pace for Lamborghini's racing models which were to include a high-performance Gallardo.

by capitalising on our brand character: aggressive, design-orientated, exclusive and typically Italian. Our target is to become a strong player on the world scene by reaching a total production capacity of at least 2,000 cars per year during the lifecycle of our present product range. Naturally we will be ready to jump on any opportunity that might lead us to even more ambitious programmes."

Greco made his clear his ambitions for Lamborghini in motorsport. The manufacturer's first entrant in endurance racing was the Murcièlago R-GT, introduced at the 2003 Frankfurt motor show and jointly developed by Audi Sport and Reiter Engineering of Germany.

To meet GT racing regulations, it was rear-wheel drive only and powered by a 6-litre non-turbo engine. The Murcielago R-GT, which weighs 1100k, was offered to anyone wanting to compete in the GT or American Le Mans series. Lamborghini quoted the purchase price as under 500,000 euros ($600,000/£335,000).

In early 2004, there was speculation that Lamborghini would mount a challenge at Le Mans in 2005. In June, 2003, Bentley (also part of Volkswagen group) took the first two places at the French 24-hour race, marking a return to success at the classic after a 70-year gap.

On its first outing, at Valencia in Spain in April 2004, the Murcielago R-GT led for much of the race and finished third. This was the first success for a competitive Lamborghini

Opening up: the Murciélago Roadster continues Lamborghini's 12-cylinder convertible tradition which began with the 350 GTS and included Miura and Diablo.

since its endurance racer came fifth in South Africa in 1986.

Greco said: "We are now starting to build this car for the many customers who have followed - with sympathy but impatience - our development work. I am sure we will see many more heated battles on the racing field of Europe, USA and Japan, where many private teams will challenge the most qualified competitors."

Lamborghini was also, during the first half of 2004, developing a racing Gallardo to compete in mono-marque competitions and other classes.

The motor racing ambitions had been clear since a night in February, 2002, when the Murciélago took three international speed records on a circuit at the Prototipo car proving centre in Nardo, Italy. Between 10.21pm and 11.21pm, in a strong south-easterly wind, a standard production Murciélago covered 305.041km (189.543 miles).

Driven by development test driver Giorgio Sanna, the car also completed 100km and 100 miles from a standing start at average speeds of 320.023km/h (198.853mph) and 320.254km/h (198.996mph) respectively. It took the Murciélago only 30 minutes and 9 seconds to cover 100 miles.

Then, in January 2003, Dr Werner Mischke was appointed chairman of Lamborghini Automobili and the Audi board of management announced that he would continue to be its member responsible for all group motorsport activities.

Lamborghini's racing ambitions continue to be on the sea as well as the land. During its first five years, Audi invested in the future of Lamborghini's powerboat engines as well as its cars, and a new building was opened in 2003 to house Motori Marini Lamborghini Spa.

The Spirit of Norway, which won the 2003 world offshore championship, was powered by Lamborghini, which is exploring other possibilities for using its power units and transmissions on water.

In 2001, Spirit of Norway won the Time Trial Championship while Victory 7 took the World Offshore Championship. Each was powered by Lamborghini's 12-cylinder, 8.2-litre marine engine.

More than 400 marine engines have been built since Ferruccio, in 1968, equipped a

Record breaker: a standard production Murciélago set three international speed records in February 2002 at Italy's Prototipo car proving centre at Nardo.

CHAPTER 09

Baglietto boat with the original sea-going engine, known as the P401. It was derived from Lamborghini's 400GT car.

Giuseppe Greco, Lamborghini Automobili's chief executive officer, has an interest in performance craft, and likes to spend time on his motor boat which he keeps in the south of Italy. He also holds a pilot's licence.

Greco's competitive edge is in tune with the enduring spirit of Sant'Agata and Ferruccio would surely have approved of his enthusiasms. Audi's man is a champion of Lamborghini's essential link between heritage and modern technology, the need to keep faith with the past, while driving hard for future success.

In the words of Giuseppe Greco: "Lamborghini spirit is still, as 40 years ago, under the sign of the Fighting Bull."

In the black: Lamborghini was confident in 2004 that the aggressively-styled Murciélago Roadster would contribute to a profitable future.

Appendix_Technical Specifications

350 GTV

First built 1963 _ Number built: 1

Engine	Front-mounted V12 60-degree aluminium block with pressed-in liners
Bore and stroke	77/62mm
Cubic capacity	3464cc
Compression ratio	9.5/1
Maximum power	360bhp at 8000rpm
Distribution	Dual overhead camshafts, chain drive, 2 valves per cylinder
Fuel system	Dual electric Bendix pumps, 6 Weber 36 IDLI carburettors
Ignition	2 coils and 2 distributors
Lubrication	Dry sump
Transmission	Rear-wheel drive
Clutch	Dry single-plate, hydraulically operated
Gearbox	ZF 5-speed
Chassis	Tubular
Suspension	Independent front and rear, coil springs and telescopic shock absorbers
Brakes	Discs to all wheels
Wheelbase/front/rear tracks	2450/1380/1380mm
Tyres	Pirelli 205/15
Dry weight	980kgs
Top speed	174mph/280km/h

350 GT

First built 1964_Number built: 120

Engine	Front-mounted V12 60-degree aluminium block with pressed-in liners
Bore and stroke	77/62mm
Cubic capacity	3464cc
Compression ratio	9.5/1
Maximum power	320bhp at 7000rpm
Distribution	Dual overhead camshafts, chain drive, 2 overhead valves per cylinder
Fuel system	Dual electric Bendix pumps, 6 Weber 40 DCOE carburettors
Ignition	2 coils and 2 distributors
Lubrication	Wet sump
Transmission	Rear-wheel drive
Clutch	Dry single plate, hydraulically operated
Gearbox	ZF 5-speed
Chassis	Tubular
Suspension	Independent front and rear, coil and telescopic shock absorbers
Brakes	Discs to all wheels
Wheelbase/front/rear tracks	2550/1380/1380mm
Tyres	Pirelli 205/15
Dry weight	1,200kgs
Top speed	155mph/250km/h

3500 GTZ (Zagato)

First built 1965_Number built: 2

Engine	Front-mounted V12 60-degree aluminium block with pressed-in liners
Bore and stroke	77/62mm
Cubic capacity	3464cc
Compression ratio	9.5/1
Maximum power	320bhp at 7000rpm
Distribution	Dual overhead camshafts, chain drive, 2 overhead valves per cylinder
Fuel system	Dual electric Bendix pump, 6 Weber 40 DCOE carburettors
Ignition	2 coils and 2 distributors
Lubrication	Wet sump
Transmission	Rear-wheel drive
Clutch	Dry single plate
Gearbox	ZF 5-speed
Chassis	Tubular
Suspension	Independent front and rear, coil springs and telescopic shock absorbers
Brakes	Discs to all wheels
Wheelbase/front/rear tracks	2550/1380/1380mm
Tyres	Pirelli 205/15
Dry weight	1050kgs
Top speed	162mph/260km/h

350 GTS

First built 1965_Number built: 2

Engine	Front-mounted V12 60-degree aluminium block with pressed-in liners
Bore and stroke	77/62mm
Cubic capacity	3464cc
Compression ratio	9.5/1
Maximum power	320bhp at 7000rpm
Distribution	Dual overhead camshafts, chain drive, 2 overhead valves per cylinder
Fuel system	Dual electric Bendix pump, 6 Weber 40 DCOE carburettors
Ignition	2 coils and 2 distributors
Lubrication	Wet sump
Transmission	Rear-wheel drive
Clutch	Dry single plate, hydraulically operated
Gearbox	ZF 5-speed
Chassis	Tubular
Suspension	Independent front and rear, coil springs and telescopic shock absorbers
Brakes	Discs to all wheels
Wheelbase/front/rear tracks	2550/1380/1380mm
Tyres	Pirelli 205/15
Dry weight	1200kgs
Top speed	155mph/250km/h

400 GT

First built 1966_Number built 273

(250 400 GT 2+2 and 23 400 GT 2-seater)

Engine	Front-mounted V12 60-degree aluminium block with pressed-in liners
Bore and stroke	82/62mm
Cubic capacity	3929cc
Compression ratio	9.5/1
Maximum power	320bhp at 6500rpm
Distribution	Dual overhead camshafts, chain drive, 2 valves per cylinder
Fuel system	Dual electric Bendix pump, 6 Weber 40 DCOE carburettors
Ignition	2 coils and 2 distributors
Lubrication	Wet sump
Transmission	Rear-wheel drive
Clutch	Dry single plate, hydraulically operated
Gearbox	Lamborghini 5-speed
Chassis	Tubular
Suspension	Independent front and rear, coil springs and telescopic shock absorbers
Brakes	Discs to all wheels
Wheelbase/front/rear tracks	2550/1380/1380mm
Tyres	Pirelli 210/15
Dry weight	1250kgs
Top speed	155mph/250km/h

400 GT Flying Star II

First built 1966_Number built: 1

Engine	Front-mounted V12 60-degree aluminium block with pressed-in liners
Bore and stroke	77/62mm
Cubic capacity	3929cc
Compression ratio	9.5/1
Maximum power	320bhp at 6500rpm
Distribution	Dual overhead camshafts, chain drive, 2 overhead valves per cylinder
Fuel system	Dual electric Bendix pump, 6 Weber 40 DCOE carburettors
Ignition	2 coils and 2 distributors
Lubrication	Wet sump
Transmission	Rear-wheel drive
Clutch	Dry single plate, hydraulically operated
Gearbox	Lamborghini 5-speed
Chassis	Tubular
Suspension	Independent front and rear, coil springs and telescopic shock absorbers
Brakes	Discs to all wheels
Wheelbase/front/rear tracks	2550/1380/1380mm
Tyres	Pirelli 210/15
Dry weight	1300kgs
Top speed	155mph/250km/h

Miura P400

First built 1966_Number built: 474

Engine	Rear-mounted V12 60-degree light alloy block with built-in gearbox and differential and pressed-in liners
Bore and stroke	82/62mm
Cubic capacity	3929cc
Compression ratio	9.5/1
Maximum power	350bhp at 7000rpm
Distribution	Dual overhead camshafts, chain drive and 2 overhead valves per cylinder
Fuel system	Dual electric Bendix pumps, 6 Weber 40 IDA 30 carburettors
Ignition	2 coils and 2 distributors
Lubrication	Wet sump
Transmission	Rear-wheel drive
Clutch	Dry single plate, hydraulically operated
Gearbox	Lamborghini 5-speed
Chassis	Unitised
Suspension	Independent front and rear, parallelogram arms, coil springs and telescopic shock absorbers
Brakes	Discs to all wheels
Wheelbase/front/rear tracks	2504/1412/1412mm
Tyres	Pirelli 205/15
Dry weight	980kgs
Top speed	174mph/280km/h

Marzal

First built 1967_Number built: 1

Engine	Rear-mounted 6 cylinders in-line, light alloy block with pressed-in liners
Bore and stroke	82/62mm
Cubic capacity	1965cc
Compression ratio	9.2/1
Maximum power	175bhp at 6800 rpm
Distribution	Dual overhead camshafts, chain drive, 2 overhead valves per cylinder
Fuel system	Dual electric Bendix pumps, 3 Weber 40 DCOE carburettors
Ignition	Coil and distributor
Lubrication	Dry sump
Transmission	Rear-wheel drive
Clutch	Dry single plate, hydraulically operated
Gearbox	Lamborghini 5-speed
Chassis	Unitised
Suspension	Independent front and rear, coil springs and telescopic shock absorbers
Brakes	Discs to all wheels
Wheelbase/front/rear tracks	2620/1480/1480mm
Tyres	Pirelli 205/14
Dry weight	1200kgs
Top speed	149mph/240km/h

Islero

First built 1968_Number built: 125

Engine	Front-mounted V12 60-degree light alloy and aluminium block with pressed-in liners
Bore and stroke	82/62mm
Cubic capacity	3929cc
Compression ratio	10.5/1
Maximum power	350bhp at 7500rpm
Distribution	Dual overhead camshafts, chain drive, 2 overhead valves per cylinder
Fuel system	Electric Bendix pumps, 6 Weber 40 DCOE carburettors
Ignition	2 coils and 2 distributors
Lubrication	Wet sump
Transmission	Rear-wheel drive
Clutch	Dry single plate
Gearbox	Lamborghini 5-speed
Chassis	Unitised
Suspension	Independent front and rear, coil springs and telescopic shock absorbers
Brakes	Discs to all wheels
Wheelbase/front/rear tracks	2550/1380/1380mm
Tyres	Pirelli 205 VR15
Dry weight	1240kgs
Top speed	155mph/250km/h

Espada 400 GT

First built 1968 _ Number built: 1

Engine	Front-mounted V12 60-degree light alloy block with pressed-in liners
Bore and stroke	82/62mm
Cubic capacity	3929cc
Compression ratio	9.5/1
Maximum power	325bhp at 6500rpm
Distribution	Dual overhead camshafts, chain drive, 2 overhead valves per cylinder
Fuel system	Electric Bendix pumps, 6 Weber 40 DCOE carburettors
Ignition	2 coils and 2 distributors
Lubrication	Wet sump
Transmission	Rear-wheel drive
Clutch	Dry single plate, hydraulically operated
Gearbox	Lamborghini 5-speed
Chassis	Unitised
Suspension	Independent front and rear, parallelogram arms, coil springs and telescopic shock absorbers
Brakes	Ventilated discs to all wheels
Wheelbase/front/rear tracks	2650/1490/1490mm
Tyres	Pirelli 205/15
Dry weight	1480kgs
Top speed	152mph/245km/h

Miura Roadster P400 (Zinc special)

First built 1968_Number built: 1

Engine	Rear-mounted V12 60-degree light alloy block, with built-in gearbox and differential, and pressed-in liners
Bore and stroke	77/62mm
Cubic capacity	3929cc
Compression ratio	9.5/1
Maximum power	350bhp at 7000rpm
Distribution	Dual overhead camshafts, chain drive, 2 overhead valves per cylinder
Fuel system	Electric Bendix pump, 6 Weber 40 IDA 30 carburettors
Ignition	2 coils and 2 distributors
Lubrication	Wet sump
Transmission	Rear-wheel drive
Clutch	Dry single plate, hydraulically operated
Gearbox	Lamborghini 5-speed
Chassis	Unitised
Suspension	Independent front and rear, parallelogram arms, coil springs and telescopic shock absorbers
Brakes	Discs to all wheels
Wheelbase/front/rear tracks	2504/1412/1412mm
Tyres	Pirelli 205/15
Dry weight	1000kgs
Top speed	174mph/280km/h

Miura S P400

First built 1968_Number built: 140

Engine	Rear-mounted V12 60-degree light alloy block with built-in gearbox and differential and pressed-in liners
Bore and stroke	82/62mm
Cubic capacity	3929cc
Compression ratio	10.4/1
Maximum power	370bhp at 7000rpm
Distribution	Dual overhead camshafts, chain drive, 2 overhead valves per cylinder
Fuel system	Electric Bendix pump, 4 triple-stroke Weber 40 IDL-3L carburettors
Ignition	2 coils and 2 distributors
Lubrication	Wet sump, common engine-transmission lubricant
Transmission	Rear-wheel drive
Clutch	Dry, single plate, hydraulically operated
Gearbox	Lamborghini 5-speed
Chassis	Unitised
Suspension	Independent front and rear parallelogram arms, coil springs and telescopic shock absorbers
Brakes	Discs to all wheels (ventilated from the second series)
Wheelbase/front/rear tracks	2500/1412/1412mm
Tyres	Pirelli HS-GR70 VR15
Dry weight	1040kgs
Top speed	177mph/285km/h

Islero S

First built 1969_Number built: 100

Engine	Front-mounted V12 60-degree light alloy block with pressed-in liners
Bore and stroke	82/62mm
Cubic capacity	3929cc
Compression ratio	10.8/1
Maximum power	350bhp at 7700rpm
Distribution	Dual overhead camshafts, chain drive, 2 overhead valves per cylinder
Fuel system	Electric Bendix pumps, 6 Weber 40 DCOE carburettors
Ignition	2 coils and 2 distributors
Lubrication	Wet sump
Transmission	Rear-wheel drive
Clutch	Dry single plate, hydraulically operated
Gearbox	Lamborghini 5-speed
Chassis	Unitised
Suspension	Independent front and rear, parallelogram arms, coil springs and telescopic shock absorbers
Brakes	Discs to all wheels
Wheelbase/front/rear tracks	2550/1380/1380mm
Tyres	Pirelli 205/15 (70 VR15)
Dry weight	1460kgs
Top speed	162mph/260km/h

Espada 400 GTE

First built 1970_Number built: 1,217 (whole series)

Engine	Front-mounted V12 60-degree light alloy block with pressed-in liners
Bore and stroke	82/62mm
Cubic capacity	3929cc
Compression ratio	10.7/1
Maximum power	350bhp at 7500rpm
Distribution	Dual overhead camshafts, chain drive, 2 overhead valves per cylinder
Fuel system	Electric Bendix pump, 6 Weber 40 DCOE carburettors
Ignition	2 coils and 2 distributors
Lubrication	Wet sump
Transmission	Rear-wheel drive
Clutch	Dry single plate, hydraulically operated
Gearbox	Lamborghini 5-speed
Chassis	Unitised
Suspension	Independent front and rear, parallelogram arms, coil springs and telescopic shock absorbers
Brakes	Ventilated discs to all wheels
Wheelbase/front/rear tracks	2650/1490/1490mm
Tyres	Pirelli 205/15
Dry weight	1635kgs
Top speed	155mph/250km/h

Jarama 400 GT

First built 1970_Number built: 177

Engine	Front-mounted V12 60-degree light alloy block with pressed-in liners
Bore and stroke	82/62mm
Cubic capacity	3929cc
Compression ratio	10.7/1
Maximum power	350bhp at 7500rpm
Distribution	Dual overhead camshafts, chain drive, 2 overhead valves per cylinder
Fuel system	Electric Bendix pump, 6 Weber 40 DCOE carburettors
Ignition	2 coils and 1 distributor
Lubrication	Wet sump
Transmission	Rear-wheel drive
Clutch	Dry single plate, hydraulically operated
Gearbox	Lamborghini 5-speed
Chassis	Unitised body
Suspension	Independent front and rear, parallelogram arms, coil springs and telescopic shock absorbers
Brakes	Discs to all wheels
Wheelbase/front/rear tracks	2380/1490/1490kgs
Tyres	Michelin 215 VR70
Dry weight	1450kgs
Top speed	162mph/260km/h

Urraco P250

First built 1970_Number built: 520

Engine	Rear-mounted V8 90-degree light alloy block with built-in gearbox and differential and pressed-in liners
Bore and stroke	86/53mm
Cubic capacity	2462cc
Compression ratio	10.4/1
Maximum power	220bhp at 7850rpm
Distribution	Overhead camshaft with cog-belt, 2 overhead valves per cylinder
Fuel system	Electric Bendix pumps, 4 Weber 40 IDFI carburettors
Ignition	2 coils and 1 distributor
Lubrication	Wet sump
Transmission	Rear-wheel drive
Clutch	Dry single plate, hydraulically operated
Gearbox	Lamborghini 5-speed
Chassis	Floor plate incorporated into the body
Suspension	Independent front and rear McPherson, coil springs and telescopic shock absorbers
Brakes	Ventilated discs to all wheels
Wheelbase/front/rear tracks	2450/1460/1460mm
Tyres	Michelin 205/14
Dry weight	1,100kgs
Top speed	149mph/240km/h

Jota

First built 1970_Number built: 1

Engine	Rear-mounted V12 60-degree light alloy block with built-in gearbox and differential and pressed-in liners
Bore and stroke	82/62mm
Cubic capacity	3929cc
Compression ratio	11.5/1
Maximum power	440bhp at 8500rpm
Distribution	Dual overhead camshaft, chain drive, 2 overhead valves per cylinder
Fuel system	Electric Bendix pumps, 4 Weber 46 IDL carburettors
Ignition	2 coils and 2 distributors
Lubrication	Dry sump with 2 pumps and radiator
Transmission	Rear-wheel drive
Clutch	Borg & Beck triple disc, hydraulically operated
Gearbox	Lamborghini 5-speed with ZF self-locking differential
Chassis	Unitised body
Suspension	Independent front and rear, parallelogram arms, coil springs and telescopic shock absorbers
Brakes	Ventilated discs to all wheels
Wheelbase/front rear tracks	2505/1410/1540mm
Tyres	Dunlop Racing: front 9/15, rear 12/15
Dry weight	900kgs
Top speed	186mph+/300km/h+

Miura SV P400

First built 1971_Number built: 150

Engine	Rear-mounted V12 60-degree light alloy block with built-in gearbox and differential and pressed-in liners
Bore and stroke	82/62mm
Cubic capacity	3929cc
Compression ratio	10.7/1
Maximum power	385bhp at 7850rpm
Distribution	Dual overhead camshafts, chain drive, 2 overhead valves per cylinder
Fuel system	Electric Bendix pump, 4 Weber 46 IDL carburettors
Ignition	2 coils and 2 distributors
Lubrication	Wet sump (dry sump to order)
Transmission	Rear-wheel drive
Clutch	Dry single plate, hydraulically operated
Gearbox	Lamborghini 5-speed
Chassis	Unitised body
Suspension	Independent front and rear, parallelogram arms, coil springs and telescopic shock absorbers
Brakes	Ventilated discs to all wheels
Wheelbase/front rear tracks	2504/1412/1541mm
Tyres	Michelin or Pirelli: front 7L/15, rear 9L/15
Dry weight	1245kgs
Top speed	186mph/300km/h

Countach LP 500

First built 1971_Number built: 1

Engine	Rear-mounted (longitudinally) V12 60-degree light alloy block with pressed-in liners
Bore and stroke	85/73mm
Cubic capacity	4971cc
Compression ratio	10.5/1
Maximum power	440bhp at 7500rpm
Distribution	Dual overhead camshafts, chain drive, 2 overhead valves per cylinder
Fuel system	Dual electric Bendix pumps, 6 Weber 45 DCOE carburettors
Ignition	2 coils and 2 distributors
Lubrication	Wet sump
Transmission	Rear-wheel drive
Clutch	Dry single plate, hydraulically operated
Gearbox	Lamborghini 5-speed
Chassis	Mixed construction (steel floor plate, aluminium sections)
Suspension	Independent front and rear, parallelogram arms, coil springs and telescopic shock absorbers
Brakes	Ventilated discs to all wheels
Wheelbase/front/rear tracks	2450/1500/1520mm
Tyres	Michelin: front 7/14, rear 9/14
Dry weight	1130kgs
Top speed	186mph+/300km/h+

Jarama 400 GTS

First built 1972_Number built: 150

Engine	Front-mounted V12 60-degree light alloy block, pressed-in liners
Bore and stroke	82/62mm
Cubic capacity	3929cc
Compression ratio	10.7/1
Maximum power	365bhp at 7500rpm
Distribution	Dual overhead camshafts, chain drive, 2 overhead valves per cylinder
Fuel system	Electric Bendix pumps, 6 Weber 40 DCOE carburettors
Ignition	2 coils and 1 distributor
Lubrication	Wet sump
Transmission	Rear-wheel drive
Clutch	Dry single plate, hydraulically operated
Gearbox	Lamborghini 5-speed
Chassis	Unitised body
Suspension	Independent front and rear, parallelogram arms, coil springs and telescopic shock absorbers
Brakes	Ventilated discs to all wheels
Wheelbase/front/rear tracks	2380/1010/1095mm
Tyres	Michelin 215/15
Dry weight	1460kgs
Top speed	162mph/260kgs

Countach LP 400

First built 1973_Number built: 150

Engine	Rear-mounted (longitudinally) V12 60-degree light alloy block with pressed-in liners
Bore and stroke	82/62mm
Cubic capacity	3929cc
Compression ratio	10.5/1
Maximum power	375bhp at 8000rpm
Distribution	Dual overhead camshafts, chain drive, 2 overhead valves per cylinder
Fuel system	Dual electric Bendix pumps, 6 Weber 45 DCOE carburettors
Ignition	2 coils and 1 distributor
Lubrication	Wet sump
Transmission	Rear-wheel drive
Clutch	Dry single plate, hydraulically operated
Gearbox	Lamborghini 5-speed
Chassis	Tubular
Suspension	Independent front and rear, parallelogram arms, coil springs and telescopic shock absorbers
Brakes	Ventilated discs to all wheels
Wheelbase/front/rear tracks	2450/1500/1520mm
Tyres	Michelin: front 205/14, rear 215/14
Dry weight	1055kgs
Top speed	196mph+/315km/h+

Urraco P200

First built 1974_Number built: 66

Engine	Rear-mounted, 8-cylinder light alloy block with built-in gearbox and differential and pressed-in liners
Bore and stroke	77/53mm
Cubic capacity	1973cc
Compression ratio	8.6/1
Maximum power	182bhp at 7500rpm
Distribution	Overhead camshafts, with cog belt drive, 2 overhead valves per cylinder
Fuel system	Electric Bendix pumps, 4 Weber 40 DCNF carburettors
Ignition	2 coils and 1 distributor
Lubrication	Wet sump
Transmission	Rear-wheel drive
Clutch	Dry single plate, hydraulically operated
Gearbox	Lamborghini 5-speed
Chassis	Floor plate incorporated into body
Suspension	Independent front and rear McPherson strut, coil springs and telescopic shock absorbers
Brakes	Ventilated discs to all wheels
Wheelbase/front/rear tracks	2450/1450/1470mm
Tyres	Michelin: front 195/14, rear 205/14
Dry weight (kerb)	1250kgs
Top speed	137mph/220km/h

Urraco P300

First built 1974_Number built: 190

Engine	Rear-mounted V8 90-degree light alloy block with built-in gearbox and differential and pressed-in liners
Bore and stroke	86/64.5mm
Cubic capacity	2996cc
Compression ratio	10/1
Maximum power	260bhp at 7000rpm
Distribution	Dual overhead camshafts, chain drive, 2 overhead valves per cylinder
Fuel system	Dual electric Bendix pumps, 4 Weber 40 DCNF carburettors
Ignition	2 coils and 1 distributor
Lubrication	Wet sump
Transmission	Rear-wheel drive
Clutch	Dry single plate, hydraulically operated
Gearbox	Lamborghini 5-speed
Chassis	Floor plate incorporated into body
Suspension	Independent front and rear, McPherson strut, coil springs and telescopic shock absorbers
Brakes	Ventilated discs to all wheels
Wheelbase/front/rear tracks	2450/1450/1470mm
Tyres	Michelin: front 195/14, rear 205/14
Dry weight	1280kgs
Top speed	162mph+/260km/h+

Bravo P114

First built 1974_Number built: 1

Engine	Rear-mounted V8 90-degree light alloy block with built-in gearbox and differential and pressed-in liners
Bore and stroke	86/64.5mm
Cubic capacity	2996cc
Compression ratio	10/1
Maximum power	300bhp at 7800rpm
Distribution	Dual overhead camshafts, chain drive, 2 overhead valves per cylinder
Fuel system	Single electric Bendix pump, 4 Weber 40 DCNF
Ignition	2 coils and 1 distributor
Lubrication	Wet sump
Transmission	Rear-wheel drive
Clutch	Dry single plate, hydraulically operated
Gearbox	Lamborghini 5-speed
Chassis	Floor plate incorporated into body
Suspension	Independent front and rear, McPherson strut, coil springs and telescopic shock absorbers
Brakes	Ventilated discs to all wheels
Wheelbase/front/rear tracks	2250/1472/1539mm
Tyres	Michelin: front 195-50/15, rear 276-40/15
Dry weight	1085kgs
Top speed	162mph/260km/h

Silhouette

First built 1976_Number built: 55

Engine	Rear-mounted V8 90-degree light alloy block with built-in gearbox and differential and pressed-in liners
Bore and stroke	86/64.5mm
Cubic capacity	2996cc
Compression ratio	10/1
Maximum power	250bhp at 7500rpm
Distribution	Dual overhead camshafts, chain drive, 2 overhead valves per cylinder
Fuel system	Single electric Bendix pump, 4 Weber 40 DCNF
Ignition	2 coils and 1 distributor
Lubrication	Wet sump
Transmission	Rear-wheel drive
Clutch	Dry single plate, hydraulically operated
Gearbox	Lamborghini 5-speed
Chassis	Floor plate
Suspension	Independent front and rear, McPherson strut, coil springs and telescopic shock absorbers
Brakes	Ventilated discs to all wheels
Wheelbase/front/rear tracks	2450/1484/1532mm
Tyres	Pirelli P7: front 195-50 VR15, rear 285-40 VR15
Dry weight	1375kgs
Top speed	162mph/260km/h

Cheetah

First built 1977_Number built: 1

Engine	Rear-mounted Chrysler V8
Bore and stroke	101.6/90.9mm
Cubic capacity	5898cc
Compression ratio	9.8/1 (unconfirmed)
Maximum power	183bhp at 4000rpm
Distribution	Push rods and rocker arms
Fuel system	Electric Bendix pump, one four-barrel carburettor
Ignition	1 coil and 1 distributor
Lubrication	Wet sump
Transmission	Four-wheel drive
Clutch	Dry single plate, hydraulically operated
Gearbox	Automatic 3-speed
Chassis	Tubular
Suspension	Independent front and rear, coil springs and telescopic shock absorbers
Brakes	Ventilated discs to all wheels
Wheelbase/front/rear tracks	3000/1520/1520mm
Tyres	Goodyear tubeless (no further information available)
Dry weight	2042kgs
Top speed	108mph/167km/h

Countach LP400 S

First built 1978_Number built: 237

Engine	Rear-mounted V12 60-degree light alloy block with pressed-in liners
Bore and stroke	82/62mm
Cubic capacity	3929cc
Compression ratio	10.5/1
Maximum power	353bhp at 7500rpm
Distribution	Dual overhead camshafts, chain drive, 2 overhead valves per cylinder
Fuel system	Electric Bendix pump, 6 Weber 45 DCOE carburettors
Ignition	2 coils and 1 distributor
Lubrication	Wet sump
Transmission	Rear-wheel drive
Clutch	Dry single plate, hydraulically operated
Gearbox	Lamborghini 5-speed
Chassis	Tubular
Suspension	Independent front and rear, parallellograms, coil springs and telescopic shock absorbers
Brakes	Ventilated discs to all wheels
Wheelbase/front/rear tracks	2450/1492/1606mm
Tyres	Pirelli P7: front 205-50/15, rear 345-35/17
Dry weight	1200kgs
Top speed	177mph/285km/h

Athon

First built 1980_Number built: 1

Engine	Rear-mounted V8 90-degree light alloy block with built-in gearbox and differential and pressed-in liners
Bore and stroke	86/64.5mm
Cubic capacity	2996cc
Compression ratio	10/1
Maximum power	250bhp at 7500rpm
Distribution	Dual overhead camshafts, chain drive, 2 overhead valves per cylinder
Fuel system	Electric Bendix pump, 4 Weber 40 DCNF carburettors
Ignition	2 coils and 1 distributor
Lubrication	Wet sump
Transmission	Rear-wheel drive
Clutch	Dry single plate, hydraulically operated
Gearbox	Lamborghini 5-speed
Chassis	Floor plate
Suspension	Independent front and rear, McPherson struts, coil springs and telescopic shock absorbers
Brakes	Ventilated discs to all wheels
Wheelbase/front/rear tracks	2450/1484/1532mm
Tyres	Pirelli P7: front 8/15, rear 11/15
Dry weight	1260kgs
Top speed	162mph/260km/h

Jalpa 350

First built 1981_Number built: 421

Engine	Rear-mounted V8 90-degree light alloy block with built-in gearbox and differential and pressed-in liners
Bore and stroke	86/75mm
Cubic capacity	3480cc
Compression ratio	10/1
Maximum power	255bhp at 7000rpm
Distribution	Dual overhead camshafts, chain drive, 2 overhead valves per cylinder
Fuel system	Electric Bendix pump, 4 Weber 42 DCNF carburettors
Ignition	Electronic with distributor and coil
Lubrication	Wet sump
Transmission	Rear-wheel drive
Clutch	Dry single plate, hydraulically operated
Gearbox	Lamborghini 5-speed
Chassis	Floor plate
Suspension	Independent front and rear, McPherson struts, coil springs and telescopic shock absorbers
Brakes	Ventilated discs to all wheels
Wheelbase/front/rear tracks	2450/1500/1554mm
Tyres	Pirelli P7: front 205-55/16, rear 255-50/16
Dry weight	1510kgs
Top speed	154mph/248km/h

LM001

First built 1981_Number built: 1

Engine	Rear-mounted AMC V8 5900cc (also tested with Lamborghini 4754cc engine)
Bore and stroke	Not available
Cubic capacity	5900cc
Compression ratio	Not available
Maximum power	180bhp at 4000rpm (AMC V8)/332bhp at 6000rpm
Distribution	Push rods and rocker arms
Fuel system	Mechanical pump, 1 4-barrel carburettor
Ignition	1 coil and 1 distributor
Lubrication	Wet sump
Transmission	Four-wheel drive
Clutch	Dry single plate, hydraulically operated
Gearbox	Chrysler A727 automatic with torque convertor
Chassis	Tubular
Suspension	Front and rear oscillating arms, torsion bars and telescopic shock absorbers
Brakes	Ventilated discs to all wheels
Wheelbase/front/rear tracks	2950/1615/1615mm
Tyres	Mix of Goodyear and Michelin 14/16 LT during testing
Dry weight	2100kgs
Top speed	100-112mph/160-180km/h (estimated)

LMA002

First built 1982_Number built: 1

Engine	Front-mounted V12 60-degree light alloy block with pressed-in liners
Bore and stroke	85.5/69mm
Cubic capacity	4754cc
Compression ratio	9.2/1
Maximum power	332bhp at 6000rpm
Distribution	Dual overhead camshafts, chain drive
Fuel system	Single electric pump, 6 Weber carburettors
Ignition	1 coil and 1 distributor
Lubrication	Wet sump
Transmission	Four-wheel drive
Clutch	Dry single plate, hydraulically operated
Gearbox	ZF S5 5-speed
Chassis	Tubular
Suspension	Independent front and rear, oscillating arms, coil springs and telescopic shock absorbers
Brakes	ventilated discs to all wheels
Wheelbase/front/rear tracks	3000/1615/1615mm
Tyres	Goodyear 14/16 LP
Dry weight	2600kgs
Top speed	117mph/188km/h

Countach LP 500 S

First built 1982_Number built: 321

Engine	Rear-mounted V12 60-degree light alloy block with pressed-in liners
Bore and stroke	85.5/69mm
Cubic capacity	4754cc
Compression ratio	9.2/1
Maximum power	375bhp at 7000rpm
Distribution	Dual overhead camshafts, chain drive, 2 overhead valves per cylinder
Fuel system	Electric Bendix pump, 6 Weber 45 DCOE carburetors
Ignition	Electronic with distributor
Lubrication	Wet sump
Transmission	Rear-wheel drive
Clutch	Dry single plate, hydraulically operated
Gearbox	Lamborghini 5-speed
Chassis	Tubular
Suspension	Independent front and rear, parallelogram arms, coil springs and telescopic shock absorbers
Brakes	Ventilated discs to all wheels
Wheelbase/front/rear tracks	2459/1492/1606mm
Tyres	Pirelli P7: front 205-50/15, rear 345-35/15
Dry weight	1490kgs
Top speed	186mph/300km/h

LM 004/7000

First built 1983_Number built: 1

Engine	Front-mounted V12 60-degree light alloy block with pressed-in liners
Bore and stroke	Not available
Cubic capacity	7000cc
Compression ratio	Not available
Maximum power	420bhp at 4500rpm
Distribution	Dual overhead camshafts, chain drive
Fuel system	Single electric pump, 6 Weber carburettors
Ignition	1 coil and 1 distributors
Lubrication	Wet sump
Transmission	Four-wheel drive
Clutch	Dry single plate, hydraulically operated
Gearbox	ZF S5 5-speed plus reduction gear
Chassis	Tubular
Suspension	Independent front and rear, oscillating arms, coil springs and telescopic shock absorbers
Brakes	Front ventilated discs, rear drums
Wheelbase/front/rear tracks	3000/1615/1615mm
Tyres	Pirelli Scorpion 325-75/VR17
Dry weight	2600kgs
Top speed	128mph/206km/h

LM002

First built 1986_Number built: 301	
Engine	Front-mounted V12 60-degree light alloy block with pressed-in liners
Bore and stroke	85.5/75mm
Cubic capacity	5167cc
Compression ratio	9.5/1
Maximum power	450bhp at 6800rpm
Distribution	Dual overhead camshafts, chain drive, 4 valves per cylinder
Fuel system	2 electric pumps, 6 Weber carburettors
Ignition	Electronic with distributor
Lubrication	Wet sump
Transmission	Four-wheel drive, front disconnecting axle
Clutch	Dry single plate, hydraulically operated
Gearbox	ZF S5 5-speed plus reduction gear
Chassis	Tubular with riveted aluminium panels
Suspension	Independent front and rear, oscillating arms, coil springs and telescopic shock absorbers
Brakes	Front ventilated discs, rear drums
Wheelbase/front/rear tracks	3000/1615/1615mm
Tyres	Pirelli Scorpion 325-65/VR17
Dry weight	2700kgs
Top speed	130mph/210km/h

Countach Quattrovalvole

First built 1985_Number built: 618	
Engine	Rear-mounted V12 60-degree light alloy block with pressed-in liners
Bore and stroke	85.5/75mm
Cubic capacity	5167cc
Compression ratio	9.5/1
Maximum power	455bhp at 7000rpm
Distribution	Dual overhead camshafts, chain drive, 4 overhead valves per cylinder
Fuel system	Two Bendix electric pumps, 6 Weber 44 DCNF carburettors
Ignition	Electronic with distributor
Lubrication	Wet sump
Transmission	Rear-wheel drive
Clutch	Dry single plate, hydraulically operated
Gearbox	Lamborghini 5-speed
Chassis	Tubular
Suspension	Independent front and rear, parallelogram arms, coil springs and telescopic shock absorbers
Brakes	Self-ventilating discs to all wheels
Wheelbase/front/rear tracks	2500/1536/1606mm
Tyres	Pirelli P7F: front 225-50 VR15, rear 345-35 VR15
Dry weight	1490kgs
Top speed	184mph/297km/h

Countach Evoluzione

1987_Number built: 1	
Engine	Rear-mounted V12 60-degree light alloy block with pressed-in liners
Bore and stroke	85.5/75mm
Cubic capacity	5167cc
Compression ratio	9.5/1
Maximum power	490bhp at 7000rpm
Distribution	Dual overhead camshafts, chain drive, 4 overhead valves per cylinder
Fuel system	Bendix electric pumps, 6 Weber 44 DCNF carburettors
Ignition	Electronic with distributor
Lubrication	Wet sump
Transmission	Rear-wheel drive
Clutch	Dry single plate, hydraulically operated
Gearbox	Lamborghini 5-speed
Chassis	Carbon fibre central structure with reinforced honeycomb panels
Suspension	Independent front and rear, parallelogram arms, coil springs and telescopic shock absorbers
Brakes	Self-ventilating discs to all wheels
Wheelbase/front/rear tracks	2500/1536/1606mm
Tyres	Pirelli P7F: front 225-50 VR15, rear 345-35 VR15
Dry weight	980kgs
Top speed	205mph/330km/h

Countach Anniversary

1988_Number built: 657

Engine	Rear-mounted V12 60-degree light alloy block with pressed-in liners
Bore and stroke	85.5/75mm
Cubic capacity	5167cc
Compression ratio	9.5/1
Maximum power	455bhp at 7000rpm
Distribution	Dual overhead camshafts, chain drive, 4 overhead valves per cylinder
Fuel system	2 Bendix electric pumps, 6 Weber 44 DCNF carburettors
Ignition	Electronic with distributor
Lubrication	Wet sump
Transmission	Rear-wheel drive
Clutch	Dry single plate, hydraulically operated
Gearbox	Lamborghini 5-speed
Chassis	Tubular
Suspension	Independent front and rear, parallelogram arms, coil springs and telescopic shock absorbers
Brakes	Self-ventilating discs to all wheels
Wheelbase/front/rear tracks	2500/1536/1606mm
Tyres	Pirelli P Zero: front 225-50 ZR15, rear 345/35 ZR15
Dry weight	1490kgs
Top speed	183mph/295km/h

Diablo

First built 1990_Number built: 2,097 (including VT)

Engine	Rear-mounted, V12 60-degree light alloy block with pressed-in liners
Bore and stroke	87/80mm
Cubic capacity	5707cc
Compression ratio	10/1
Maximum power	492bhp at 6800rpm
Distribution	Dual overhead camshafts, chain drive, 4 overhead valves per cylinder
Fuel system	2 Bendix electric pumps, Lamborghini electronic sequential multipoint injection system
Ignition	Electronic injection integrated
Lubrication	Wet sump
Transmission	Rear-wheel drive
Clutch	Dry single plate, hydraulically operated
Gearbox	Lamborghini 5-speed
Chassis	Tubular
Suspension	Independent front and rear arms, coil springs and coaxial telescopic shock absorbers
Brakes	Self-ventilating discs to all wheels
Wheelbase/front/rear tracks	2650/1540/1640mm
Tyres Pirelli:	front 245-40 ZR17, rear 335/35 ZR17
Dry weight	1490kgs
Top speed	183mph/295km/h

Diablo VT

First built 1992_Number built: 2,097 (including Diablo 1990-98)

Engine	Rear-mounted, V12 60-degree light alloy block with pressed-in liners
Bore and stroke	87/80mm
Cubic capacity	5707cc
Compression ratio	10/1
Maximum power	492bhp at 6800rpm
Distribution	Dual overhead camshafts, chain drive, 4 overhead valves per cylinder
Fuel system	2 Bendix electric pumps, Lamborghini electronic sequential multipoint injection system
Ignition	Electronic injection integrated
Lubrication	Wet sump
Transmission	Four-wheel drive
Clutch	Dry single plate, hydraulically operated
Gearbox	Lamborghini 5-speed
Chassis	Tubular
Suspension	Independent front and rear arms, coil springs and coaxial telescopic shock absorbers
Brakes	Self-ventilating discs to all wheels
Wheelbase/front/rear tracks	2650/1540/1640mm
Tyres	Pirelli P Zero: front 245-40 ZR17, rear 335/35 ZR17
Dry weight	1735kgs
Top speed	202mph/325km/h

Diablo SE

First built 1993_Number built: 150

Engine	Rear-mounted, V12 60-degree light alloy block with pressed-in liners
Bore and stroke	87/80mm
Cubic capacity	5707cc
Compression ratio	10/1
Maximum power	520bhp at 7100rpm
Distribution	Dual overhead camshafts, chain drive, 4 overhead valves per cylinder
Fuel system	2 Bendix electric pumps, Lamborghini electronic sequential multipoint injection system
Ignition	Electronic injection integrated
Lubrication	Wet sump
Transmission	Rear-wheel drive
Clutch	Dry single plate, hydraulically operated
Gearbox	Lamborghini 5-speed
Chassis	Tubular
Suspension	Independent front and rear arms, coil springs and coaxial telescopic shock absorbers
Brakes	Self-ventilating discs to all wheels
Wheelbase/front/rear tracks	2650/1540/1640mm
Tyres Pirelli:	front 235-40 ZR17, rear 335-30 ZR18
Dry weight	1490kgs
Top speed	205mph/330km/h

Diablo Roadster

First built 1995_Number built: 85

Engine	Rear-mounted, V12 60-degree light alloy block with pressed-in liners
Bore and stroke	87/80mm
Cubic capacity	5707cc
Compression ratio	10/1
Maximum power	492bhp at 7000rpm
Distribution	Dual overhead camshafts, chain drive, 4 overhead valves per cylinder
Fuel system	2 Bendix electric pumps, Lamborghini electronic sequential multipoint injection system
Ignition	Electronic injection integrated
Lubrication	Wet sump
Transmission	Four-wheel drive
Clutch	Dry single plate, hydraulically operated
Gearbox	Lamborghini 5-speed
Chassis	Tubular
Suspension	Independent front and rear arms, coil springs and coaxial telescopic shock absorbers
Brakes	Self-ventilating discs to all wheels
Wheelbase/front/rear tracks	2650/1540/1640mm
Tyres	Pirelli: front 235-40 ZR17, rear 335-35 ZR17
Dry weight	1625kgs
Top speed	201mph/323km/h

Diablo SV

First built 1996_Number built: 184

Engine	Rear-mounted, V12 60-degree light alloy block with pressed-in liners
Bore and stroke	87/80mm
Cubic capacity	5707cc
Compression ratio	10/1
Maximum power	500bhp at 7000rpm
Distribution	Dual overhead camshafts, chain drive, 4 overhead valves per cylinder
Fuel system	2 Bendix electric pumps, Lamborghini electronic sequential multipoint injection system
Ignition	Electronic injection integrated
Lubrication	Wet sump
Transmission	Rear-wheel drive
Clutch	Dry single plate, hydraulically operated
Gearbox	Lamborghini 5-speed
Chassis	Tubular
Suspension	Independent front and rear arms, A-arms, coil springs and coaxial telescopic shock absorbers (double on rear axle)
Brakes	Self-ventilating discs to all wheels
Wheelbase/front/rear tracks	2650/1540/1640mm
Tyres	Pirelli: front 235-40 ZR17, rear 335-30 ZR18
Dry weight	1450kgs
Top speed	186mph/300km/h

Diablo SVR

1996_Number built: 50

Engine	Rear-mounted, V12 60-degree light alloy block with pressed-in liners
Bore and stroke	87/80mm
Cubic capacity	5707cc
Compression ratio	10/1
Maximum power	540bhp at 7100rpm
Distribution	Dual overhead camshafts, chain drive, 4 overhead valves per cylinder
Fuel system	2 Bendix electric pumps, Lamborghini electronic sequential multipoint injection system
Ignition	Electronic injection integrated
Lubrication	Wet sump
Transmission	Rear-wheel drive
Clutch	Dry single plate, hydraulically operated
Gearbox	Lamborghini 5-speed
Chassis	Tubular
Suspension	Independent front and rear arms, A-arms, coil springs and coaxial telescopic shock absorbers (double on rear axle)
Brakes	Self-ventilating discs to all wheels
Wheelbase/front/rear tracks	2650/1540/1640mm
Tyres	Pirelli: front 235/615/18, rear 335/675 ZR 18
Dry weight	1485kgs
Top speed	186mph/300km/h

Diablo SV Roadster

1998_Number built: 34

Engine	Rear-mounted, V12 60-degree light alloy block with pressed-in liners
Bore and stroke	87/80mm
Cubic capacity	5707cc
Compression ratio	10/1
Maximum power	530bhp at 7100rpm
Distribution	Dual overhead camshafts, chain drive, 4 overhead valves per cylinder
Fuel system	2 Bendix electric pumps, Lamborghini electronic sequential multipoint injection system
Ignition	Electronic injection integrated
Lubrication	Wet sump
Transmission	Rear-wheel drive
Clutch	Dry single plate, hydraulically operated
Gearbox	Lamborghini 5-speed
Chassis	Tubular
Suspension	Independent front and rear arms, A-arms, coil springs and coaxial telescopic shock absorbers (double on rear axle)
Brakes	Self-ventilating discs to all wheels
Wheelbase/front/rear tracks	2650/1540/1640mm
Tyres	Pirelli: front 235-40 ZR17, rear 335-30 ZR18
Dry weight	1450kgs
Top speed	over 186mph/300km/h

Diablo GT

First built 1999_Number built: 80

Engine	Rear-mounted V12 60-degree light alloy block with magnesium intake manifold, mid (longitudinally) mounted
Bore and stroke	87/84mm
Cubic capacity	5992cc
Compression ratio	10.7/1
Maximum power	575bhp at 7300rpm
Distribution	Dual overhead camshafts, chain drive, 4 overhead valves per cylinder
Fuel system	Lamborghini electronic sequential multipoint injection system
Ignition	Static with individual coils
Lubrication	Wet sump
Transmission	Rear-wheel drive
Clutch	Dry single plate
Gearbox	Lamborghini 5-speed
Chassis	Tubular
Suspension	Independent front and rear A-arms, coil springs, anti-roll bar and electronically-controlled shock absorbers
Brakes	Self-ventilating discs to all wheels
Wheelbase/front/rear tracks	2650/1650/1670mm
Tyres	Pirelli: front 245-35 ZR18, rear 335-30 ZR18
Dry weight	1490kgs
Top speed	199mph – 210mph/320 - 338 km/h (varied according to gear ratios, options and rear-wing configuration)

Diablo GTR
1999_Number built: 30

Engine	Rear-mounted V12 60-degree light alloy block with magnesium intake manifold, mid (longitudinally) mounted
Bore and stroke	87/84mm
Cubic capacity	5992cc
Compression ratio	10.7/1
Maximum power	509bhp at 7300rpm
Distribution	Dual overhead camshafts, chain drive, 4 valves per cylinder
Fuel system	Lamborghini electronic sequential multipoint injection system
Ignition	Static with individual coils
Lubrication	Wet sump
Transmission	Rear-wheel drive
Clutch	Dry single plate
Gearbox	Lamborghini 5-speed
Chassis	Tubular
Suspension	Independent front and rear A-arms, coil springs, adjustable anti-roll bar and electronically controlled shock absorbers
Brakes	Self-ventilating discs to all wheels
Wheelbase/front/rear tracks	2650/1650/1670mm
Tyres	Pirelli: front 245/645 18, rear 325/705 18
Dry weight	1400kgs
Top speed	210mph/338km/h

Diablo 6.0
2000_Number built: 383 (including 45 SE)

Engine	Mid- (longitudinally-) mounted V12 60-degree light alloy block with magnesium intake manifold
Bore and stroke	87/84mm
Cubic capacity	5992cc
Compression ratio	10.7/1
Maximum power	550bhp at 7100rpm
Distribution	Dual overhead camshafts, chain drive, 4 valves per cylinder
Fuel system	Lamborghini electronic sequential multipoint injection system
Ignition	Static with individual coils
Lubrication	Wet sump
Transmission	Four-wheel drive
Clutch	Dry single plate
Gearbox	Lamborghini 5-speed
Chassis	Tubular
Suspension	Independent front and rear A-arms, coil springs, anti-roll bar and electronically-controlled shock absorbers
Brakes	Self-ventilating discs to all wheels
Wheelbase/front/rear tracks	2650/1610/1670mm
Tyres	Pirelli: front 235/35 Z18, rear 335/ZR18
Dry weight	1625kgs
Top speed over	205mph/330km/h

Murciélago
First built 2001_Number built: 935 (to end 2003)

Engine	Rear-mounted longitudinal V12 60-degree aluminium alloy light alloy block
Bore and stroke	87/86.8mm
Cubic capacity	6192cc
Compression ratio	10.7/1
Maximum power	580bhp at 7500rpm
Distribution	Dual overhead camshafts, 48 valves, electronically-controlled intake and exhaust variable valve timing
Fuel system	Lamborghini electronic sequential multipoint injection system
Ignition	Static with individual coils
Lubrication	Forced, with pump mounted inside gearbox
Transmission	Four-wheel drive
Clutch	Dry, single plate
Gearbox	Lamborghini 6-speed
Chassis	Tubular
Suspension	Double front and rear oscillating arms, anti-roll bars and electronically-controlled shock absorbers
Brakes	Power vacuum, H (hydraulic) system with ABS+DRP (dynamic rear proportioning), aluminium-alloy four-cylinder calipers
Wheelbase/front/rear tracks	2665/1635/1695mm
Tyres	Pirelli: front 245/35 ZR18, rear 335/30 ZR18
Dry weight	1650kgs
Top speed	205mph/330km/h

Gallardo

First built 2003_Number built (to end 2003) 933

Engine	Rear-mounted longitudinal V10 90-degree aluminium alloy light alloy block with 4 overhead camshafts and 4 valves per cylinder
Bore and stroke	82.5x92.8mm
Cubic capacity	4961cc
Compression ratio	11/1
Maximum power	500bhp at 7800rpm
Distribution	Dual overhead camshafts and chain drive
Fuel system	Lamborghini electronic system, fuel-injected
Ignition	Lamborghini electronic system
Lubrication	Forced, with pump mounted inside gearbox
Transmission	Four-wheel drive
Clutch	Double plate
Gearbox	Lamborghini 6-speed (electronic change optional)
Chassis	Structural aluminium space frame
Suspension	Double wishbones front and rear, FSD shock absorbers
Brakes	Ventilated discs to all wheels with ABS
Wheelbase/front/rear tracks	2550/1622/1592mm
Tyres	Pirelli P Zero: front 235/35 ZR19, rear 295/30 ZR19
Dry weight	1430kgs
Top speed	192mph/309km/h

Murciélago Roadster

First built: 2004_Number built: production due from summer 2004

Engine	Rear-mounted longitudinal V12 60-degree aluminium alloy light alloy block
Bore and stroke	87/86.8mm
Cubic capacity	6192cc
Compression ratio	10.7/1
Maximum power	580bhp at 7500rpm
Distribution	Dual overhead camshafts, 48 valves, electronically-controlled intake and exhaust variable valve timing
Fuel system	Lamborghini electronic sequential multipoint injection system
Ignition	Static with individual coils
Lubrication	Forced, with pump mounted inside gearbox
Transmission	Four-wheel drive
Clutch	Dry, single plate
Gearbox	Lamborghini 6-speed
Chassis	Tubular
Suspension	Double front and rear oscillating arms, anti-roll bars and electronically-controlled shock absorbers
Brakes	Power vacuum, H (hydraulic) system with ABS+DRP (dynamic rear proportioning), aluminium-alloy four-cylinder calipers
Wheelbase/front/rear tracks	2665/1635/1695mm
Tyres	Pirelli: front 245/35 ZR 18, rear 335/30 Z8 18
Dry weight	1650kgs
Top speed	205mph/330km/h

Index

Adams, Tim, 115
Alfa Romeos, 12, 22, 28
Alfieri, Guilio, 64, 68, 69, 86, 97
Aliot, Philippe, 97
Andretti, Mario, 101
Audetto, Danielle, 78, 79, 88, 93, 98
Audi, 78, 129, 131, 133-142, 144, 146, 148, 151, 153, 156, 158
Automobili Lamborghini Spa, 22, 46, 48, 83, 88, 113, 115, 116, 118, 136, 137, 141
Baldi, Mario, 79
Baraldini, Franco, 59
Bertone, Nuccio, 33, 36-39, 42, 58, 65, 139
Bizzarrini, Giotto, 22, 23, 24
Braner, Robert A., 116
Campelini, Luigi, 59, 61
Car magazine, 156, 158
Carreras, Jose, 101
Ceccarani, Massimo, 86, 125
Chrysler, 85-88, 93, 104, 109, 133-135, 138
Clark, Jim, 11
Clarkson, Jeremy, 130
Condivi, Mario, 12
Curtis, Steve, 78
DaimlerChrysler, 133, 134
Dallara, Giampaolo, 22, 27 -30, 33, 40, 41
De Tomaso, 40, 41, 86
Delmas, Yanack, 97
Dennis, Ron, 111
Detroit auto show, 127, 155
Di Capua, Vittorio, 125-127, 129-131, 137, 141
Djodi, Setjawan, 116-118
Donckerwolke, Luc, 139-142, 148, 156
Donnelly, Martin, 97

Eaton, Bob, 113
Eduardo, Don, 33
Ferrari, Enzo, 7, 18, 22
Ferrari models
    246 Dino, 42
    250 GT, 7
    250 GTO, 22, 23
    275, 27
    308 GTB, 53
    328, 87
    F40, 90
    Testarossa, 54
Ferraris, Franco, 86
Forghieri, Mauro, 87, 88, 100
Formula One, 41, 87, 88, 97-100, 116
Frankfurt motor show, 94, 143, 155, 158
Gaglioti, Dominico, 78
Gale, Bob, 94
Gallerani, Seb, 78
Gandini, Marcello, 30, 42, 36, 37, 39, 92, 93
General Motors, 118
Geneva motor show, 26, 27, 30, 33, 38, 42, 48, 53, 65, 70, 74, 107, 123, 125, 129, 130, 143, 153, 155, 157
Girotti, Giuseppe, 98, 110
Gordon-Stewart, Nigel, 118
Greco, Giueseppe, 158, 159, 162, 166
Guigiaro, Giorgetto, 123
Hakkinen, Mika, 111
Harrah, Bill, 59
Hill, Graham, 11
HR Owen, 122
Iacocca, Lee, 85-88, 93, 94, 100, 101
International Lead Zinc Research Organization (ILZRO), 39
    Zn 75, 39
Jolliffe, David, 12, 79
Kimberley, Mike, 115, 117-119, 123-125
Lamborghini, Bruciatori, 18, 20, 49

Lamborghini, Ferruccio, 6, 7, 9, 11-13,
    15-18, 20- 24, 26-30, 34, 35, 37, 38, 41,
    44-46, 48, 51, 52, 64, 75, 79, 93, 112
Lamborghini, Tonino, 35, 49
Lamborghini models
    350 GT, 8, 9, 12-15, 20, 24-27, 36, 40,
        115, 170
    350 GTS, 171
    350 GTV, 18, 19, 24, 26, 30, 170
    350 GTZ, 170
    350 Roadsters, 35
    400 GT, 27, 28, 33, 35-39, 171
    400 GT Flying Star II, 171
    Athon, 179
    Bravo, 100, 105, 107, 108
    Bravo P114, 177
    Cheetah, 61, 62, 70, 178
    Countach, 46-48, 58, 62, 74, 82, 83
    Countach 400S, 64, 69, 74
    Countach 500S, 67, 74
    Countach Anniversary, 182
    Countach Evoluzione, 83, 181
    Countach LP 400, 48, 51, 52, 54, 176
    Countach LP 400S, 178
    Countach LP 500, 52, 176
    Countach LP 500S, 54, 180
    Countach Quattrovalvole, 72, 79, 81, 181
    Diablo, 82, 88, 91-94, 96, 100, 101,
        103-105, 107, 108, 115
    Diablo 6.0, 185
    Diablo GT, 184
    Diablo GTR, 134, 143, 185
    Diablo Roadster, 116, 183
    Diablo SE, 108, 112, 117, 183
    Diablo SV, 120, 124, 125, 136, 137, 183
    Diablo SVR, 124, 125, 184
    Diablo SV Roadster, 125, 128, 143, 184
    Diablo VT, 182
    Espada, 41, 42, 46, 52, 53, 57, 58, 60,
        156
    Espada 400 GT, 38, 40, 41, 173
    Espada 400 GTE, 174
    Flying Star, 36
    Gallardo, 148-151, 153, 156, 158, 186
    Islero, 41, 42, 46, 172
    Islero S, 41, 174
    Jalpa, 69, 81, 82, 90
    Jalpa 350, 76, 79, 179
    Jarama, 53, 60
    Jarama 400 GT, 16, 17, 41, 42, 174
    Jarama 400 GTS, 79, 52, 176
    Jarama GTS, 57
    Jarama P400 GTS, 46
    LM001, 179
    LM002, 70, 73-75, 81, 88, 96, 97, 122,
        129, 158, 181
    LM004/7000, 180
    LMA002, 180
    Marzal, 36, 38, 172
    Miura, 53, 57
    Miura P400 SV, 45
    Miura Roadster P400, 39, 41, 172, 173
    Miura S, 41, 44
    Miura S P400, 173
    Miura S Jota, 44, 45, 57, 175
    Miura Spider, 39
    Miura SV, 42, 45, 52
    Miura SV P400, 175
    Miura V12, 20, 28-30, 33, 35
    Monza 400, 36
    Murciélago, 144, 146-148, 151, 153, 156,
        185
    Murciélago R-GT, 154, 155, 160, 161
    Murciélago Roadster, 156, 157, 160, 162,
        166, 185
    P140 Cala, 91, 107, 108, 123, 128
    P147 Raptor, 127, 141
    P250 Urraco, 52, 53
    P300 Urraco, 64
    P350 Jalpa, 75

P400, 28, 30
Raptor, 125, 128, 129, 137-139
Silhouette, 60, 64, 178
Urraco, 42, 44, 46, 48, 52, 53, 58, 60
Urraco P200, 177
Urraco P250, 175
Urraco P300, 57, 177
Lamborghini Tractors, 16, 17, 48
Lauda, Nikki, 88
Le Mans, 9, 79, 124, 140, 161
Legendary Car magazine, 22
Leimer, Rene, 51, 52, 54, 57-60, 62, 64, 65
Levy, Carl, 93
Lotus Cortina, 11, 12
Lotus Elan, 41, 42
Lutz, Bob, 86
Marazzi, Mario, 36, 38
Marmaroli, Luigi, 68, 74, 86, 95
Maserati, 64, 68, 86
Megatech, 118, 119, 122, 133-135, 141, 146
Mimran family, 68, 69, 79, 93, 112
Mimran, Jean-Claude, 64, 67
Mimran, Patrick, 64, 67, 78-82
Mobility Technology International (MTI), 61, 62
Monte Carlo, 101
Moss, Stirling, 7, 8
Motor Industry Research Agency (MIRA), 60
Munari, Sandro, 87, 94, 126
Nastase, Joe, 73
Novaro, Emile, 68, 69, 78, 79, 86, 88, 91, 93, 94, 101, 105, 110, 112
Patrucco, Carlo, 100
Philips, Roger, 12
Piëch, Dr. Ferdinand, 136, 139, 151
Poole, Larini, 100
Poole, Van Der, 100
Porsche, 122, 131
Portofino, 95

Reti, Zoltan, 64
Ricard, Paul, 97
Richards, Tony, 86, 93, 97, 105, 107, 111, 112
Rocchio, Rodolfo, 137
Rolt, Tony, 9
Rossetti, Georges-Henri, 46, 51, 52
Royce, Mike, 110, 115
S.A.M.E, 48
Sant'Agata, 35-37, 39, 41, 42, 48, 53, 57, 61, 65, 68, 74, 83, 88, 90, 91, 94, 95, 98-101, 104, 108, 110-112, 115, 117, 118, 124-126, 129, 133, 135, 137, 138, 140-143, 146-148, 151, 153, 166
Sargiotto Bodyworks, 24
Scaglione, Franco, 24, 26
Senna, Ayrton, 111
Setright, LJK, 22, 23
Sgarzi, Ubaldo, 12, 13, 26, 27, 30, 33, 39, 49, 68, 70, 86, 104, 105, 110
Simister, John, 22
Smith, Bob, 86, 93
Spice Engineering, 79
Stanzani, Paolo, 13, 22, 28-30, 37, 41, 42, 44, 46, 52, 92
Stevens, Peter, 118
Sucharto, Tommy, 113, 117, 118, 125-127, 129, 131
Supercar Classics magazine, 23
Timor Car, 127, 129
Top Gear magazine, 130
Touring Bodyworks, 26, 27
Turin motor show, 29, 42, 54, 69, 95
Venturelli, Gianfranco, 86, 116, 126
Wallace, Bob, 7-12, 20, 28, 35, 44
Warwick, Derek, 97
Wheels magazine, 38
Woolf, Walter, 12, 62, 64
World War II, 15, 16, 73
Zagato, 125
Zampoli, Claudio, 92

Acknowledgements

Most of the people mentioned in this book assisted me with my research and I would like to make special mention and give my thanks to the following:

Dr. Giuseppe Greco, Automobili Lamborghini Spa
Cristina Guizzardi, Automobili Lamborghini Spa
Ubaldo Sgarzi, former Lamborghini sales manager
Stefan Pasini, Lamborghini author and historian
Danielle Audetto, managing director, Lamborghini Engineering
Emile Novaro, former managing director, Automobili Lamborghini
Anthony Richards, Chrysler
My wife Carole for her valued contribution in drafting the book and
finally my close friend Mark Jackson who has encouraged me tremendously during the writing of the book.

Automobili Lamborghini Spa was especially helpful in providing photographic images. Other photographs were provided by Haymarket LAT, and there is one picture from my own archive.

David Jolliffe